the police & the community

The Committee for Economic Development is an independent research and educational organization of two hundred businessmen and educators. CED is nonprofit, nonpartisan, and nonpolitical and is supported by contributions from business, foundations, and individuals. Its objective is to promote stable growth with rising living standards and increasing opportunities for all.

All CED policy recommendations must be approved by the Research and Policy Committee, a group of sixty trustees, which alone can speak for the organization. In connection with the publication of Statements on National Policy, CED often publishes studies prepared by scholars as background papers and deemed worthy of wider circulation because of their contribution to the understanding of a public problem. The opinions and conclusions expressed in such papers are solely those of the individual authors and do not necessarily reflect the policies or views of the trustees.

The studies in this volume relate to the Research and Policy Committee's 1972 policy statement, *Reducing Crime and Assuring Justice.* They have been approved for publication as Supplementary Paper Number 36 by an editorial board of trustees and advisors. They also have been read by the members of the Advisory Board of the Committee for the Improvement of Management in Government, who have the right to submit individual memoranda of comment for publication.

robert f. steadman, editor

the police & the community

bernard l. garmire
jesse rubin
james q. wilson

A Supplementary Paper of the
Committee for Economic Development

THE JOHNS HOPKINS UNIVERSITY PRESS
Baltimore and London

The Johns Hopkins University Press, Baltimore, Maryland 21218
The Johns Hopkins University Press Ltd., London

Library of Congress Catalog Card Number 72-84

ISBN 0-8018-1412-X (clothbound edition)
ISBN 0-8018-1413-8 (paperback edition)

Originally published, 1972
Johns Hopkins Paperbacks edition, 1972

contents

foreword

This country has an extremely serious crime problem. There also are grave problems with the attitudes, conduct, and management of the nation's police. These problems are interconnected, although too great a share of responsibility for crime control ought not be placed upon the police; the courts, prosecution patterns, and correctional methods carry great weight in the administration of criminal justice. Nor should the police be held accountable for changes in the mores of a heterogeneous population undergoing rapid urbanization, modifications in basic life-styles, and the consequences of sweeping technological transformations.

The broad range of governmental functions concerned with crime and justice, including the criminal codes, is dealt with in the Committee for Economic Development's policy statement, *Reducing Crime and Assuring Justice.** The focus of the three

*Reducing Crime and Assuring Justice, a Statement on National Policy by the Research and Policy Committee, Committee for Economic Development (New York: June 1972)

background papers here presented is upon the relationship between urban police forces and the people who reside in the inner core areas of great cities. Outside the scope of these studies are the roles of the 3,000 elective county sheriffs and their deputies, the 50,000 state troopers and patrolmen, the 35,000 officers employed by the national government to secure enforcement of its laws, or the fragmented local police forces of suburban areas. This is not to ignore the very real problems that exist in these areas but rather to assert the crucial nature of the police-people relationships in the central cities.

Major crimes of violence reported per 100,000 inhabitants are five to eight times greater in the central cities than in suburban and rural areas. Major offenses against property are also far higher. And in inner core areas these ratios become almost astronomical. Victimization rates reach levels that justify the fears of those residents who hesitate to venture outside their doors, and of others who refuse to enter such neighborhoods. The desire for protection of persons and property is strongly felt in these places, where relationships between residents and police are under constant strain. The national Capitol, the White House, and the United Nations headquarters are located in or near such areas; indeed, there is no major city in this country where the quality of life is unaffected to some degree by these conditions.

The three authors whose views are bound together in this text bring exceptional qualifications to bear on this most vital field of inquiry. They approach the subject from different professional backgrounds, while sharing an unusual depth of experience. Bernard L. Garmire is widely known as one of the nation's ablest and most thoughtful chiefs of police, with thirty years of experience in four major cities. Dr. Jesse Rubin is a psychiatrist who has conducted intensive studies of the interpersonal relationships with which we are concerned. And James Q. Wilson, Professor of Government at Harvard University, has become the preeminent authority on police administration among political scientists through long years of distinguished and perceptive research. The insights and judgments of these men form a dependable basis for corrective action.

Emerging from their analyses is a sense of need—an imperative need—for closer harmony and mutual support between the great majority of inner-city inhabitants and the local police. It is made clear that constructive cooperation of a high order will require changes of attitude and conduct on both sides of this equation. The public will have to offer assistance and moral support *to* the police as well as demanding aid from them. And the police must learn to act in ways that elicit respect rather than distrust or disapprobation. It is easier to define the necessary changes, of course, than to find effective ways of bringing them about—which is what the authors have sought to do and have succeeded in doing.

The police should be more interested in gaining popular approval through improvement of their methods and operations than most forces have shown themselves to be. The police self-image appears to be quite negative; most officers, of all ranks, seem to feel that their efforts are not well regarded or fully appreciated. Some carry this so far that they develop persecution complexes, verging on paranoia. Social contacts tend to be limited, in the main, to other police officers and their families. Prof. Wilson notes the fact that researches find far more support and appreciation for police, even in slum-ghetto areas and among populations regarded as hostile, than either the police are aware of or the general public might expect. Favorable attitudes need the reenforcement that would come from visible improvements in police outlook and performance.

There is no pretense, of course, that intense hostility against the police does not exist among significant numbers of inner-city residents—most notably but not exclusively involving young male blacks. Nor is there any doubt that many police officers harbor reciprocal animosities, whether or not these feelings are suppressed in execution of their duties. Evidence mounts on both counts, most dramatically in the recent increase of unprovoked assaults upon police officers extending to assassination. Means must be found to alleviate the tensions that are at least in part responsible for such expressions of violence; few, if any national goals deserve higher priority.

Approaching these and related issues from distinctive standpoints, the three authors offer a wide variety of constructive measures designed to meet this challenge. Varied as they are, these recommendations are not mutually inconsistent. All could be pursued concurrently in their main outlines: reorganization and redeployment of urban police forces; greater care in recruitment; professionalization through training and supervision; and enhancement of cultural ties between police and the people.

Chief Garmire's emphasis upon the two contrasting or conflicting police roles—"community service" versus "crime fighting"—clearly merits organizational application, at the very least on an experimental basis. Separate recruitment criteria, separate training designs, and separate assignments for these two distinctive functions provide a hopeful prospect for a profound improvement in police-people relationships within the inner cities—and probably elsewhere, as well.

If the great majority of urban police-citizen contacts were to involve officers screened and trained to maintain a "service" posture, the historic military challenge, "Who goes there, friend or enemy?", would be less likely to elicit an unfortunate response when applied to police in the ghetto. Most residents of every category regardless of age or race want more—not less— police protection of the "maintenance of order" type. Chronic wrongdoers, steeped in criminal ways, are the minority; cures for their condition probably lie beyond the reach of the police in any case.

There is complete agreement on the need for careful screening of police recruits, to guard against tendencies toward sadism and against prejudicial attitudes that may weaken ability to maintain high standards of professional conduct in discretionary confrontations. There is no disagreement, either, with the importance of stronger recruiting efforts from among the population being policed. Specifically, blacks, Spanish-speaking people, and other minority groups should be represented on police forces in proportion to their shares of population. Further, evidence supports the desirability of area assignments where officers are indigenous, which implies that local police officers should be required to live in or near the locations they patrol.

There is an apparent conflict, however, between this concept and the view that college graduates and others with high educational qualifications should be actively recruited. Educational levels are far below average in the inner cities, and emotional resistance to appointment to police forces as presently constituted is high—most of all among higher-income residents. But two solutions are available to overcome this difficulty. Both are used in the program of Rochester, New York, where the Monroe Community College offers a special two-year collegiate curriculum in police administration, and where cadets are recruited at younger ages with encouragement to enroll for in-service college courses. A police force both indigenous and college-trained may emerge from this program.

Proper stress is laid upon the importance of a professional police outlook and professional police standards. Some cities have moved toward this goal; in others it would seem almost incongruous in view of the present composition of their forces, at both rank and file levels. But the objective is worthy of the most tenacious adherence. The individual officer in contact with the public has great discretion, which should be exercised within clearly defined and accepted professional limits. The argument is not wholly valid that physicians, teachers, attorneys, and members of some other recognized professions function without so much quasi-military discipline. The police could certainly be required to meet professional standards comparable with those of the nursing profession. At the command level, it is reasonable to insist upon even higher educational standards, including the study of management.

Vital as the foregoing proposals surely are, the nation must not lose sight of the overriding necessity for reconciliation and harmonization of interests between citizenry and police. Many additional actions would contribute to that end.

Modernization of the criminal codes, to relieve the police from enforcement of unpopular and moralistic laws against gambling and other victimless "crimes," would make it easier to stamp out the infectious corruption that has crept into so many urban forces with consequent impairment of public respect. Implementation of the "team" concept advanced by Dr. Rubin, with each team member trained in his own specialty, holds real promise. And various means are suggested for overcoming the self-imposed social isolation of police officers that reenforces their negative self-images; professional officers can surely be brought into active daily association with those elements of American society who want nothing more than to assist in bringing the scourge of major crime under control.

However useful community relations divisions may be in certain situations, it must be clear that no member of the "order-maintenance" or "community service" forces can be relieved of this kind of responsibility. Every officer represents the whole force (and all of organized society, as well) in his every contact with any citizen. He must learn, through training or otherwise, to conduct himself accordingly. The discovery that those officers who enjoy a high degree of family stability function best in these matters is not beside the point; it is directly on target.

In the crime crisis of this past decade it is not the police alone who have been found wanting. The legislative bodies, the judiciaries, correctional instrumentalities, executive official-dom—all have fallen down. The general public has been deeply at fault, calling on the one hand for more policemen and on the other hand denouncing those we have for their deficiencies, all the while refusing to give sufficient time or attention to gain some understanding of the realities involved or to search out and support constructive solutions. Most of the problems appear to be soluble—though not through carping criticism alone.

These three articles clearly reveal one central problem: we Americans have not known who the police are, or should be, or what we actually want them to do. Lacking knowledge we citizens (and the police) have accepted a mythology of police work. This has isolated the police from reality and has misdirected the help that the people intended to give them. Too often, we have seen the policeman as a crime fighter when actually there is very little that most policemen can do to combat crime. The departments are fragmented and the causes of crime are pervasive—not addressed by current police policies. We have at the same time denied and downgraded a major and legitimate aspect of the police role, that of community service, or peacekeeping. We have assumed that the main problem is "lack of professionalization," when in fact it may be too much internalization and isolation. We have rightly urged training on the police, but refused to define clearly the roles for which they are trained.

Major reforms, sweeping changes are overdue—for the police and every other agency of law enforcement. And all of these may not achieve the desired results until the social and economic conditions in areas where crime proliferates are brought up to minimum standards of housing, health, education, and employment opportunities. People of good will have work to do.

Robert F. Steadman
Director, Improvement of Management in Government, CED

the police & the community

1 bernard l. garmire
the police role in an urban society

One of the most critical issues facing the United States today is
the definition of the police role in a modern and urban demo-
cratic society. Until that role is defined, both for the present
and the future, we shall never effectively resolve the pressing
problems with which we are confronted—a very grim prospect
indeed.

The 1960's were years of great fear, discord, and strife; yet
we know that this may be only a prologue to events that would
occur in the decade we have now entered. We are all haunted by
the possibilities inherent in the violence, hatred, and fear that
beset our society; and we are equally aware of the great responsibility that falls to the police service for preventing these
possibilities from becoming reality. Here we pause fearfully. For
if the police service of the 1970's responds to the challenges and
the responsibilities of this decade as it did in the last decade,
failure is assured. We cannot escape the conclusion that in the
1960's the police were severely tried and found to be des-

perately wanting. The nation has survived this failure, but the record of the police in the 1960's has made success in the 1970's more imperative but less attainable.

As the first and activating element of the criminal justice system, the police are confronted with a multiplicity of problems, many of which are shared in common with the entire system, which is in deep difficulty. But central to these problems is a single basic issue, concerning the administration of the police service; to lose sight of this is to obscure the real crisis of policing today. In turn, any solution to this problem can only come about through a resolution of the police role or roles.

Friend of All, Armed Nemesis of Some

Historically, the roles of police, even though not carefully or accurately articulated, were nonetheless generally understood and accepted. Quite obviously, this is most definitely not the case in contemporary America. Youth, ethnic groups, academicians, political leaders, businessmen, and lay citizens all have divergent, disparate views of those historic police roles. This lack of consensus has created an atmosphere in which sharp conflict over the rationale for police action flourishes, and consequently bitter debate rages throughout a community or even the nation. These debates are sometimes so acrimonious that the only result is a tearing of the social fabric that holds a community or nation together.

History has left us a bewildering hodgepodge of contradictory roles that the police are expected to perform. We may well ask, for example, are the police to be concerned with peace-keeping or crime fighting? The blind enforcers of the law or the discretionary agents of a benevolent government? Social workers with guns or gunmen in social work? Facilitators of social change or defenders of the "faith"? The enforcers of the criminal law or society's legal trash bin? A social agency of last resort after 5:00 p.m. or mere watchmen for business and industry?

Actually, the police are expected to do all those things and become all things to all people, at once the confessor and the inquisitor, the friend of all yet the armed nemesis of some. Supermen, not men, could do all these things; but, the theory of supermen was practiced three decades ago, and the civilized world is the less for it.

In sum, the public had developed such high expectations of its police that those expectations moved beyond reality to something that could be better described as faith. As the public came to have faith in the police to do all things, the police came to have faith that they could do all things; when disillusionment set in, the singers lost faith in the song, in each other, and in themselves.

If we are to restore any semblance of faith in the police by the public—and the police themselves—we must begin first by defining the police role very carefully so that it does not distort reality. The historical definition of the police role eventually achieved this regrettable result by fostering the belief that police, because they were present and visible twenty-four hours a day, could function as a gigantic surrogate service agency to the community handling all the needs of the people all of the time.

To establish credibility or faith in the police service requires that the police role be delineated so that there are reasonable expectations about what the police should do and can do. Once we know what the police are to do, then we can address the three critical problems of police recruitment, training, and leadership. As matters stand now, we do not know what we are recruiting men for, what kind of training and education they ought to have, or what kind of leadership we ought to be developing—because we don't know where we want to lead them in the first place.

The result of this failure is that the police perform two conflicting basic roles that cannot be integrated administratively in any single agency. Yet operationally, individual police officers are assigned those very same conflicting roles and are expected to master them psychologically so that, in the street, they can perform each with proficiency as the occasion demands. These two roles are community service and law enforcement.

3

bernard l. garmire

I define the community-service role as one in which the police provide essentially a social service to the community; i.e., intervening in domestic quarrels, handling those who are under the influence of alcohol or drugs, working with dependent and neglected children, rendering emergency medical or rescue services and generally acting as a social agency of last resort—particularly after 5:00 p.m. and on weekends—for the impoverished, the sick, the old, and the lower socioeconomic classes.

An example of the community-service role is the family fight. What is needed here are the skills and resources of a marriage counselor, a psychiatrist, or a social worker. It does not serve the interests of either the state or the man and the wife to make an arrest. Nor does it serve the interests of the state or the family simply to suppress the noise level of the quarrel or to prevent an assault by invoking the threat of arrest and jail.

I define the law-enforcement role as one in which the police enforce criminal laws. This is the role for the crime fighter and the thief catcher. In this role, the primary tasks are criminal investigation, collection of evidence, interrogation of suspects, arrests of suspects, maintenance of order and safety, combatting organized crime, suppression of disturbances and riots, and, generally, the hard core enforcement of criminal laws.

The commission of a robbery in which the victim was brutally assaulted clearly falls within the law-enforcement role. In this case, law-enforcement and criminal-investigation skills are required to identify the suspect and to bring him before the court.

Police agencies and police officers are attempting to fill both roles, and I submit that they are not properly trained, equipped, or capable of performing *either* role with any degree of success, let alone both of them. Even if the numbers of policemen were vastly increased, even if their training were improved, and even if their resources were expanded, I still submit that they could not perform both roles—so sharply do they conflict and so different are the skills required. One person simply cannot reasonably be expected to master both roles intellectually and jump

4

psychologically from one to another in an instant's notice. Furthermore, the law-enforcement role of police is so strongly perceived by some citizens that they totally reject the idea that police could or should fill a community-service role even if they were capable of doing so.

Here is the kind of thing that we expect of today's police officer:

At 9:00 p.m. he responds to a robbery in progress and upon arrival exchanges gunshots with a suspect.

At 10:00 p.m., after he has made a report of the incident, he receives a call of a violent family brawl. He is white, they are black, and the suspect with whom he just exchanged gunfire an hour earlier was black. The officer is expected to handle their marital problems effectively and dispassionately, but he also has to return to radio service quickly because it is Saturday night and two other calls are waiting for him. Need more be said? Do we really believe that one man can do this night after night, month in and month out? Granted, the officer is not fired upon or assaulted every night. But the potential is there and he knows it: witness the frequent news reports concerning the ambushes, sniping, and other offenses directed against police. Is it not time that we took notice of the realities of policing and admit that one man or one group of men cannot intellectually and psychologically do all this?

In order to consider this question, the Miami police department collaborated with the Psychiatric Institute Foundation to study police response to stress. This study was financed by the Law Enforcement Assistance Administration (LEAA). The results of this study, which are described in the following chapter, suggest that the multiplicity of roles that officers must fill contributes significantly to police fatigue and stress. My own personal experience of thirty-three years in the police service in all ranks strongly affirms this finding.

Such studies must be regarded only as a beginning; we must explore much more fully the possibilities of developing a psychiatric set of standards for police work, which in turn poses

5

this basic question: What are the roles police perform and what are the criteria and measurement methods to identify those applicants who are best suited to perform each role or a combination of roles? We must examine the hypothesis that there is a constellation of psychological factors that makes some persons better suited for one kind of police role than another. We must determine what makes a good community-service worker, a good crime fighter, and a good administrator; we must discover, if possible, ways of finding persons who can perform adequately in two or more different roles.

Two Agencies Under Civilian Control

What is implicit in the foregoing analysis is a drastic reorganization of the administration of the police function, as suggested at the outset of this chapter. The police service must be reorganized both structurally and functionally so that it conforms in a rational way to the realities of the roles to be performed. I will outline here one organizational scheme for accomplishing this.

The contemporary police organization should be divided into two agencies under one department, one concerned with the law-enforcement function, the other with the community-service function. The community-service agency would operate on a twenty-four-hour basis and would be satisfied by people who are psychologically best suited for this function as well as specifically educated and trained to perform it. There would be no need for them to operate in uniform, and, depending on the locality generally, no need for them to be armed. They may or may not have full powers of arrest.

The law-enforcement agency would function as criminal investigators, thief catchers, and so forth, and it likewise would be composed of people psychologically attuned to the law-enforcement role and for it. In essence, they would be performing the police functions of patrol and investigation; they would, of course, be armed and possess full police powers.

6

Administering both agencies at the departmental level would be a professional staff composed of public administrators directly responsible to the elected or appointed head of government. The public administrators would not necessarily be policemen. Indeed, they should be chosen for their administrative expertise—not just for their law-enforcement or community-service expertise. The overhead or staff agencies should be predominantly staffed by civilians possessing required skills in such areas as planning, budgeting, personnel administration, and systems analysis. I wish to emphasize the importance of developing and maintaining civilian control over both the law-enforcement and community-service agencies.

The highest career professional in each agency would be a director, who reports to the public administrator. The director would have only a small administrative staff because the bulk of the staff services would be provided and controlled at the departmental level, further strengthening the concept of civilian control. In short, the law-enforcement and community-service agencies would be strictly line or operating agencies.

Additionally, a citizen advisory board should be established composed of persons appointed and elected to that board. The members should represent and be drawn from all elements of the community. This would be a board charged not with investigating civilian complaints against the police, but with the far more important responsibility of advising the department on problems, means, and goals. The board should deliberately seek to provide policy input and feedback.

It is clear that fewer personnel would be needed in the law-enforcement function than in the community-service function. Numerous studies have indicated that the greater part of a police officer's time—perhaps two-thirds—is spent in the service role rather than the enforcement role. But if we truly attempt to provide adequate community services, we must expect to increase our personnel and financial commitments in this area.

It will not be possible simply to take a police department and divide it into the two agencies without increasing both personnel and financing. I would estimate that total resources will have to be increased by 20 to 25 per cent in order to implement the new system.

I would recommend such an increase *only* if it were to be employed in establishing the new organizational complex—not if it were to be invested in the present police system. It is time that we recognized the tremendous inefficiencies that exist in the policing function. Until the police structure and function are rationalized in this country, such an investment would amount to throwing good money after bad.

It must be admitted that the new system as proposed here perhaps raises more questions than it answers. The intent is to propose a conceptual model for a new system, not to settle all the myriad details. If the concept has merit, then the details and attendant problems can be worked out during the research and testing phase.

One specific element that should be mentioned is traffic control. Even though untold resources have been diverted from the police forces in an effort to combat the traffic problem, the results have been rather meager. The basic question is whether traffic control is indeed properly a function of police, or whether traffic offenders should be handled in a criminal or quasi-criminal process. The answer may well be in handling traffic cases through a separate administrative system, with an educational and training process substituted for fines or imprisonment. For those who persistently violate the traffic codes, penalties under a point system might well be invoked, with the worst offenders being denied their driving privileges. In fact, the entire mechanism of traffic control should be removed from the criminal justice system and handled as a transportation or social-service matter. It might appropriately fall under the community-service arm of a reorganized police force.

The Need for Outside Help

No matter what new models for the reform and reorganization of the police function are chosen, it is hardly realistic to expect that the initiative for these moves are to come solely, or perhaps even mainly, from within the police forces themselves. The average police department is too ingrown, too stagnant, to undertake this kind of vigorous, sweeping action. Nor, in a sense, is it fair to place the whole burden of reform on the shoulders of the police. For the development of truly efficient police forces, organized along the functional lines suggested in this chapter, requires the creation of new governmental structures; such an endeavor lies outside either the scope or the competence of the police.

An outstanding example of such a problem—one of the most persistent and frustrating problems confronting our municipalities and states—is the Balkanization of the police forces. There are approximately 40,000 police agencies ranging in size from one man to 30,000 men. It is not necessary to elaborate on the disadvantages of such a fractured system; they are too well known. Perhaps only cities of 50,000 or more should be allowed their own police agencies; the state should police the smaller cities and the rural areas. In the metropolitan areas there should be consolidation of the smaller police agencies. If this were done, the number of police agencies could be reduced from 40,000 agencies to roughly 400-plus agencies—with clear gains in terms of effectiveness and efficiency.

The consolidation of police agencies, accompanied by a rationalization of police structure and function, could be the first step down the long road toward the reform of the police system and the resolution of its problems. But very clearly a move of such magnitude will require the combined exertions and the cooperation of many government agencies at all levels, from federal through local, as well as assistance from agencies in the private sector. This likewise applies to many other badly needed

9

reforms, which are unlikely to come through the efforts of the police alone. One such vitally important initiative is the loosening up of the present rigid parochialism of police department bureaucracies that promotes and perpetrates mediocrity and inefficiency. We must open avenues for lateral entry into police agencies, providing for movement of those with integrity and expertise from department to department, as well as some sort of a retirement system which could be transferred from place to place. Again, there is a vital need for some national system for the rating of police agencies for their effectiveness and efficiency. This would be a great improvement over the Uniform Crime Reporting system as it exists today; needless to say, the magnitude of such a system is such that only the federal government is capable of bringing it into being.

What is of the utmost importance is that a start be made—now—in implementing the concepts discussed in this chapter. Initial steps that could be taken to bring about a coordination of efforts to this end are:

First, the police service must break down its institutional version of the Berlin Wall and seek assistance and advice from nonpolice organizations, such as foundations and agencies in the psychiatric, social work, and similar fields.

Second, the federal government and foundations are in an admirable position to induce two or three municipal governments to experiment with the concepts through cash grants to support the costs and to evaluate the results.

Third, both organizations can support research and educational and training programs designed to prepare police agencies for conversion to the new system.

Fourth, private industry can assist by providing funding programs to encourage development of the new system, and, through the exercise of community leadership, it can encourage municipal and state governments to modernize and rationalize their police systems.

A recent observation by William A. Westley is apropos here. "The police," he writes, "must be given the advantage of sophisticated knowledge of social organizations which is now transforming industry and other community institutions in ways appropriate to the requirements of modern society."[1]

But even were this to be accomplished successfully, I do not believe that this will make policemen and the police service objects of love and endearment; it is not in the nature of men—particularly Americans—to give such affection to those representatives of authority who directly control their lives. And, no matter how we describe the activities of the police, the business of police is policing. The most that we can hope for, police-community relations or public relations notwithstanding, is respect for the police as professionals, confidence in their integrity, and public conviction that the police will perform their mission.

2 jesse rubin
police identity and the police role

The young police recruit, like any beginning professional, enters his career at a time of life when rapid growth, conflict, and crisis are normal aspects of his personality. After joining the force, he must work at forming his adult identity at the same time that he is learning the techniques of his profession. To both tasks, the psychological and the technical, he brings with him fixed characteristics such as physical endowment and native intelligence as well as self-image, character structure, and other attributes that are in a state of flux. Because a policeman's job is not a casual nine-to-five experience, his work will become a major, pervasive aspect of his identity as a man. Therefore, early experiences on the job will have important and relatively permanent effects on his developing adult identity. About two years after entering the force, he will have settled into a work role that will determine for better or worse the kind of policeman—

Acknowledgment: The author would like to thank Miss Gail Meltzer for research assistance in the preparation of this paper.

and the kind of man—he is to become. Should these years intensify the normal "growing pains" of young manhood, rather than to help resolve them, the cadet will fail to achieve the mature psychological integration necessary for functioning at a professional level.

Unfortunately, the formation by the young policeman of a truly professional identity is hindered by conflicts inherent in the police role itself. The interaction of the young man's personality with these role conflicts is the subject of this chapter, which is based both on a review of the literature as well as on the Miami field study of police behavior under stress, mentioned in the previous chapter. This latter study, spanning a period of more than a year, has been useful not only in delineating the psychological characteristics of the young police recruit but also in suggesting concrete ways to improve the organization of urban police forces; these are also described in this chapter.

The Miami Fatigue Study, carried on from July 1970 through September 1971 through the collaboration of the Miami Police Department and the Psychiatric Institute Foundation, investigated the interaction of stress, fatigue, and personality on police behavior.[1] In developing this study, the author and his coworkers each spent approximately fourteen hours a day for seven successive days riding in patrol cars.* The resulting observations, which covered all shifts, were recorded daily in detailed narrative form. From this initial experience, personality factors, indicators of stress and fatigue, and objective measures of behavior were derived. For example, it was determined that useful indicators of the stress induced by a radio call included speed of driving, muscle tension of hands and arms on the wheel, and changes in rate and frequency of speech. Police behavior that varied during citizen contacts included controlling and threaten-

*Daniel Cruse, Associate Professor of Psychology, University of Miami; and Charles Ferster, Professor and Chairman, Department of Psychology, American University.

ing types of behavior; behavior that involved dispensing of assistance, education, advice and counseling; and behavior involving physical aggression.

It should be emphasized that policemen themselves were used extensively in the observation process. (Among the various advantages of this procedure was that it avoided the resentment and even hostility that outside observers sometimes incur in policemen.) Fatigue could be easily self-rated on a five-point scale by policemen on duty. Four police patrolmen were trained to fill out forms that objectively rated on standardized scales the types of citizen and police behaviors described. A subject group of twelve policemen were observed by the policemen observers during their regular duty. In all, more than a thousand police-citizen contacts were observed and recorded; additionally, the twelve policemen subjects and all seventy-seven police cadets going through the police academy during the year were given standard psychological tests.*

A second project, the Miami Police-Community Interaction Program, was conducted simultaneously by the police department and the Miami Model Cities Program. In this nine-month project, supervised and evaluated by the Psychiatric Institute Foundation,[2] thirty police officers and thirty model cities residents were chosen at random to work together full time for two weeks on problems of mutual concern, with the objective of accomplishing specific tasks to solve these problems. Ten such two-week workshops were held between October 1970 and May 1971, involving a total of 300 police officers and a somewhat larger number of model cities residents.

As administrator of both these projects, I spent many hours during the last year speaking with and observing officers of all ranks in the Miami police department and working with them on

---

*Personality factors were measured by the use of screening intelligence tests (Kuhlman-Anderson), vocational interest tests (Strong Vocational Interest Blank), and a standardized pencil-and-paper, self-administered personality test (Minnesota Multiphasic Personality Inventory).

the administrative, political, and programmatic problems inherent in carrying out such complex projects.

The Miami study corroborates other recent studies in its finding that those who enter police work are generally psychologically healthy and competent young men who display common personality features that should serve them well in a police career. However, certain ambiguities, inconsistencies, and conflicts in the socially and legally sanctioned roles of the police impede optimal resolution of the identity struggle that the recruit is experiencing. There is a conflict between the peacekeeping, community-service, and crime-fighting roles of the police, as well as between the policeman's need to be an individualist and at the same time to fit into an organization and to accept discipline. There are further conflicts within the quasi-judicial and establishment-protective roles of the policeman, and the black policeman experiences an additional conflict in his role as mediator between the police and the black community.

The Miami study showed that problems between the police and the community—especially the black community—are partly due to police-role conflicts. To the extent that this is true, carefully designed programs can alleviate these problems. Specific task-oriented programs can help break the vicious circle of stereotyping and negativism inherent in police-community relations. Essential components of such programs are highly professional directors; definition of specific tasks to be pursued; commitment of adequate time, personnel, and money by the police department and the sponsoring agency; total backing of the police chief; and planning for follow-up programs.

The young policeman can be helped to achieve a professional identity through methods of deploying, training, and recruiting police. The Miami study indicates that since no policeman can concurrently fulfill all the roles expected of him, police departments should divide into several sections, each of which is assigned a clear, primary policing role. One of these would be a peacekeeping and community-service arm, as represented by neighborhood police teams. These teams should be composed of men specifically recruited and trained to accomplish such police missions as preventive patrol, community liaison, working with juvenile delinquents (both as individuals and in gangs), helping in citizen disputes, routine traffic investigation, and preventing crime. Excellence in such work would be recognized and rewarded. It is further recommended that each neighborhood team policeman be trained as a generalist-specialist in such fields as family disputes, community organization, and paramedical work, e.g., handling acute drug and alcohol intoxication and emergency first aid.

A second police arm would have as its role the primary mission of fighting crime, whenever and wherever it occurs. It would rely heavily on modern information-gathering and computer-processing techniques for deployment and strategy decisions and would work under a highly centralized command.

Because of the different role expectations for each police arm, most policemen should be recruited and trained to function in one or the other, though some men might be found who could function in either. Since these ideas have not been adequately tested, criteria for recruitment and training have not yet been established, but it is emphasized that once roles are clear, this task can be accomplished. The model presented also should make police more responsive to discipline and command.

Identity Formation in Young Manhood

Identity formation during late adolescence and early adult life has received a great deal of attention in the psychiatric literature. The aspect of identity formation most pertinent to our subject is that described by Erik H. Erikson.[3] Erikson writes that the criterion of moving from adolescence to adult life is the formation of a secure identity. The latter Erikson defines as the relatively enduring self-image of an individual that *coincides* with the reflected view of himself which he receives from those around him. This is to say that there are two important components to an adult's identity: first, an inner sense of who he is as a person and what his values, capacities, goals, and life style are; second, how his family, peers, and the community view him. If these two components are positive and congruent, identity is secure. Insofar as they are negative and incongruent, a sense of identity diffusion or conflict will occur, with consequent anxiety and stunting of psychological growth. In Erikson's words,

> The growing and developing youths . . . are . . . primarily concerned with *what they appear to be in the eyes of others as compared with what they feel they are, and with the question of how to connect the roles and skills cultivated earlier with the occupational prototypes of the day* . . . . Ego identity is . . . the ego's ability to integrate all identifications . . . with the opportunities offered in social roles. The sense of ego identity is the *accrued confidence that the inner sameness and continuity prepared in the past are matched by the sameness and continuity of one's meaning for others, as evidenced in the tangible promise of a career* . . . . The danger of this stage is *role confusion.* (Italics added.)[4]

Erikson thus emphasizes how, through work, a man can express that which is essentially himself, and he can have confirmation of this self-image from those around him.

For the young policeman, establishing this congruence is particularly difficult. The role expectations of police amplify, rather than reduce, identity problems. Given current police-role conflicts, a young policeman is vulnerable to settling into a work identity characterized by immaturity, lack of discipline, rigidity, and paranoia.

In order to examine this process in detail, we will look at the type of man who becomes a policeman, and then follow the course of his career as he attempts to master the police roles he is expected to assume.

Personality of Police Recruits

The policeman has been described as "a frustrated dictator who is attracted to the police service in order to give vent to his aggressive or neurotic feelings."[5] Though this is a view widely shared, Arthur Niederhoffer, after an extensive review of the pertinent literature, concludes that there is no evidence that

17

highly authoritarian people go into police work.[6] He finds that insofar as authoritarian trends do exist in policemen, these are more the result of acculturation on the job than of preexisting personality, and that the relationship between personality and occupational choice remains an open question.

A study by Joseph Matarazzo and his colleagues in Portland, Oregon, of successful police applicants indicates that they are characterized by high intelligence, superior personality adjustment, and an orientation toward social service—that is, they are oriented toward jobs involving working with people.[7] Robert Mills notes that police recruits represent a quiet type of community service motivation.[8] He feels that the desire for security and public approval tempers competitiveness and aggressiveness in policemen. This is supported by Nelson A. Watson and James W. Sterling, who find that two of the three reasons given by police as most important in continuing a police career are related to job security.[9]

After giving projective tests and interviews to more than 1,000 applicants for the Chicago police department, Clifton Rhead and his associates found that "the picture which unfolds, then, is of an individual who is more suspicious than the average person, one who is ready to take risks, and is prone to act on his impulses . . . . There appears to be in those persons who chose police work for a career a greater degree of paranoid ideation, a greater emphasis on virility, and a greater tendency to act out than in the nonpolice population."[10]

The results of the Miami study tend to confirm broadly all these studies. As we have noted, Matarazzo and Mills found that social or community service ranked high in the interest of police recruits.* Our impression is that young men go into police work

---

*Watson's findings are mixed in this regard. Social service aspects of the job do not rank high in his questionnaire about motives for joining the force, but his survey revealed that 86 per cent *disagreed* with the statement, "Good police work requires that officers concern themselves with the consequence of crime and not with its roots or causes."[11] I would take this as a sign of social and community concern.

with at least a moderate community-service orientation. Policemen vary, of course, in the extent to which they view community and peacekeeping activities as a positive role expectation for their work. In the course of our studies in Miami, we spoke with policemen who felt that this was an important factor in their decision to go into police work, and with others to whom it was of relatively little importance. Nevertheless, beginning officers to whom this aspect of the job is completely distasteful are rare.

By and large, the policemen we observed tend to be somewhat suspicious and cynical, as Rhead found, but not to a degree that could be called paranoid. They are assertive, have a high level of physical energy, and are restless. With regard to the latter, many officers talked about their lifelong need to discharge a lot of energy. Some liked to drive fast, often commuting long distances at high speeds; some found an outlet on the golf course; others simply described a ceaseless muscular restlessness.

Closely related to restlessness is what may be called "stimulus hunger." That is, policemen are not introspective; rather, they look to the environment for perceptual stimulation in order to maintain alertness and optimal functioning. For this reason, nearly all policemen we talked with hate routine. Many said their chief motive for joining the force was that police work offers constantly new and unpredictable stimuli, situations, and problems. The thought of being confined indoors and doing repetitive work was extemely distasteful.*

The policeman is ambivalent about authority. Though proud of his uniform and badge, he does not want command to intrude into his territory. This ambivalence is intimately tied to a specific police-role conflict, and will be dealt with in detail later in this chapter.

---

*The most recent television recruitment ads for the Washington police force stress that policemen work outdoors and are not subject to a day-to-day routine.

We did not find any consistent abnormal psychological pattern among the policemen or cadets. Several of the officers we talked with had been preoccupied in childhood with being physically undersized, and several others had a history of impulsive and mildly antisocial behavior during adolescence. (One, for example, gave a history of repetitive window breaking, speeding violations, and fighting a good deal during adolescence.) In comparing our psychological test results in Miami with those of Matarazzo, we find that in general the results are the same, though the Miami police cadets tend slightly more toward a "normal" (or at least average) personality profile than those in Portland. Both groups show some elevations in the scales (MMPI) which indicate a need for activity and also a need for the discharge of impulses. The amount of this deviation is not abnormal, but seems to confirm our direct observations that policemen are highly energetic, aggressive people. Thus, Miami policemen as a group display certain personality patterns that are not in themselves abnormal but which, under the pressures of role conflicts described later, could (and sometimes do) result in rigid, paranoid, and impulsive behavior.

What is it, then, that a young man of this type is looking for when he decides to go into police work? In response to his aggressiveness and restlessness, for example, he seeks a chance for action and an opportunity for muscular activity, and he anticipates that police work will satisfy these needs. Stimulus hunger can be harnessed into the police function of scanning the environment in order to prevent trouble. Police work also promises an outlet for his healthy suspiciousness and cynicism. (Someone who is naively accepting would probably make a very bad policeman.) Impulsivity can also be sublimated in police work—sublimated in the sense that impulsivity can be molded and matured into decisiveness, a highly prized quality among police. If a man has had conflicts over small stature, they can be resolved by the prestige and authority of wearing a uniform and carrying a weapon. Though we have not gathered any data which allows us to speculate as to whether police service gratifies unmet sexual needs or conflicts, it was our observation that policemen are seen as desirable sexual objects by many young women. Police speak of the existence of "cop-chasing broads" who are said to be ready, willing, and able to engage in sexual activities on or off duty—preferably the former.

Thus, the recruit brings certain personality traits, unfixed and in flux to his job. The optimal outcome of this occurs when, as Rhead puts it, "the ego of the successful police officer utilizes these traits in the service of normal day-to-day relationships."

Police "Professionalism" and Training

It is the psychological task of the cadet to synthesize the personality trends just described with the multiple and sometimes inconsistent roles expected of him as a policeman, and to forge all this into a work identity that we would call "professional." Since much of the following discussion hinges on the obstacles to accomplishing this, it would seem well to pause for a moment to clarify what is implied by "police professionalism."

James Q. Wilson follows Everett Hughes in noting that one characteristic of all professionals is that "they handle on a routine basis what to others are emergencies." He also notes that professionals are characterized by the exercise of "wide discretion alone and with respect to matters of the greatest importance."[12] Police certainly do this. But, he goes on,

The right to handle emergency situations, to be privy to "guilty information," and to make decisions involving questions of life and death or honor and dishonor is usually . . . conferred by an organized profession. The profession certifies that the member has acquired by *education* certain information and by *apprenticeship* certain arts and skills that render him competent to perform these functions and that he is willing to subject himself to the code of ethics and sense of duty of his colleagues. (Italics added.)[13]

Wilson notes that these criteria are not met in policing.

Niederhoffer lists nine points that characterize professions generally: high standards of admission; a special body of knowl-

21

edge and theory; altruism and dedication to the service ideal; a lengthy period of training for candidates; a code of ethics; licensing of members; autonomous control; pride of the members in their profession; and publicly recognized status and prestige.[14] Once again, police work, by and large, does not meet these criteria.

Thus, there is general agreement that a professional is someone who achieves the privilege of exercising discretion within his field of competence only through discipline, training, and apprenticeship. He must subject himself to the discipline of learning the technical principles of the profession as well as to the discipline inherent in his organizational structure. In terms of its requirements, policing is a profession, but police training generally falls very far short of coming within such a definition.

Training programs for police recruits vary enormously. Charles B. Saunders, citing a study by George W. O'Conner, notes that "less than 15 per cent of all agencies surveyed by IACP [International Association of Chiefs of Police] in 1965 provided immediate training for recruits; about half provided it 'as soon as possible,' within the first year."[15] According to the President's Commission on Law Enforcement and the Administration of Justice,

It remains doubtful whether even the majority of them [i.e., training programs] provide recruits with an ample understanding of the police task. For example, very few of the training programs . . . provide course material on the history of law enforcement, the role of police in modern society, or the need for discretion in law enforcement . . . . Current training programs, for the most part, prepare an officer to perform police work mechanically, but do not prepare him to understand his community, the police role, or the imperfections of the criminal justice system.[16]

Saunders adds, "Much of the training is poorly presented by unqualified instructors; often it is irrelevant to the realities of police work and lacking in essential background information on the principles of law enforcement and the police role in the community."[17] The result, says Niederhoffer, is that,

The new patrolman must resolve the dilemma of choosing between the professional ideal of police work he has learned at the academy and the pragmatic precinct approach. In the academy, where professionalism is accented, the orientation is toward that of the social sciences as opposed to the lock-them-up philosophy, but in the precinct the patrolman is measured by his arrest record. Thus, the new man is needled when he shows signs of diffidence in arresting or asserting his authority. Over and over again, well-meaning old timers reiterate, "Ya gotta be tough kid, or you'll never last."[18]

The police academy in Miami has not per se been a subject of our investigations. But based on its subsequent effect on police function there, and on the literature reviewed above, we would conclude that while academies may teach much that is technically valuable, they by and large do little but provide a pause or hiatus in the development of the work identity of the policeman. Certainly, nothing indicates that recruit training anticipates or helps resolve the impending work-identity crisis.

Police Role Conflicts

We will now look at how role conflict shapes the identity of the young policeman as he tries to perform six different police roles.[19] Three of these roles in particular—the three generally accepted roles of peacekeeping (or maintaining order), crime fighting, and community service—are the sources of the policeman's most difficult conflicts. In addition to these three historically defined roles, policemen also function in paramilitary, quasi-judicial, and possibly establishment-protective capacities; the conflicts and ambiguities inherent in these roles are discussed later.

The first role of the police, legally sanctioned since the origins of policing in England, has been the preservation of the peace. James S. Campbell defines the peacekeeping role this way, "This . . . duty is a broad and most important mandate which involves the protection of lives and rights ranging from handling street corner brawls to the settlement of violent family disputes. In a word, it means maintaining public safety."[20]

Although the police role which first springs to the mind of the average citizen is that of the crime fighter, this is a fairly recent addition to the function of the police. Indeed, Wilson notes that in mid-nineteenth century Boston, apprehension of thieves, robbers, and murderers was not considered to be in the province of the police at all.[21] Campbell states that "execution of this task involves what is called police operations, and this ranges from preparing stakeouts to arresting suspects."[22]

Even more recently, society began to see government generally as serving a variety of social service functions. As part of this, the police unofficially and gradually assumed the community-service role. Policemen are expected to provide emergency medical, social-welfare, and psychological services, particularly to lower-class citizens and especially on nights and weekends. Wilson notes that "service" functions may vary from "first aid, rescuing cats, helping ladies, and the like."[23]

The tensions created by these often conflicting expectations of the police function are described thus by Campbell:

Perhaps the most important source of police frustration, and the most severe limitation under which they operate, is the conflicting roles and demands involved in the order-maintenance, community-service, and crime-fighting responsibilities of the police. Here both the individual police officer and the police community as a whole find not only inconsistent public expectations and public reactions, but also inner conflict growing out of the interaction of the policeman's values, customs, and traditions with his intimate experience with the criminal element of the population. The policeman lives on the grinding edge of social conflict, without a well-defined, well-understood notion of what he is supposed to be doing there.[24]

Invariably, when the author asked a police patrolman in Miami what his job consisted of, he answered in a mechanical way, "Protection of life and property and the preservation of peace." Thus he confirmed what he had been taught in cadet school to be his primary role—that of the peacekeeper. And despite the popular conception of his job, peacekeeping does occupy him most of the time. Wilson notes that service (noncriminal) calls represented the largest single category of calls (37.5 per cent) to the Syracuse police department. They were followed in order of frequency by order-maintenance calls (30.1 per cent). Law-enforcement (crime fighting) calls constituted *only 10.3 per cent of all calls.*[25] Wallach, in a study of a Baltimore police district, demonstrated that

> the bulk of police activity . . . does not relate to the . . . crime control function. The vast majority of police activities . . . do not involve crimes and most of the crime-related contacts are really after-the-fact report-taking from crime victims . . . . The vast majority of all resident requests sampled was related to the maintenance of order, the settling of interpersonal disputes, and the need for advice and emergency assistance. Over all, crime related calls constituted *less than one-fourth* of . . . police service calls. (Italics added.)[26]

In a recent statement Chief Bernard L. Garmire of the Miami Police said, "A. . . sample of all the calls for service in 1970 disclosed that 61 per cent of the calls did not involve either serious or minor crimes; i.e., they were calls in which a citizen wanted some kind of service not related to crime per se. This, incidentally, is a conservative figure."[27]

Though the community calls mostly for community service and peacekeeping, policemen nevertheless consider the fundamental job, the "real guts" of policing, to be the apprehension of felons. In Wallach's words, "There is a sharp difference between the police emphasis on crime and most of their activities." Police are occupied with peacekeeping—but preoccupied with crime fighting.

The Frustrations of Community Service

Why are policemen least satisfied with those aspects of their work that take up most of their time, yet are most committed to the relatively least time-consuming aspect—crime fighting?*

---

*Though the peacekeeping and community service roles differ, they will be discussed together because the frustration of each occurs through the same mechanisms.

As noted earlier in this chapter, most policemen on entering the force either positively wish to fill the peacekeeping and community-service roles, or are at least willing to tolerate them as a major aspect of their work. Once on the job, however, tendencies in this direction are frustrated by a number of factors, beginning with the realization that there are no built-in rewards for good performance as a peacekeeper. Pats on the back, compliments about doing a good job, and other verbal and nonverbal rewards from the peer, supervisory, or command levels rarely follow the successful completion of a peacekeeping or community-service activity.*

Furthermore, police officers believe that citizens have little regard for their performance in the area of peacekeeping and community service. Findings from the Miami Police-Community Interaction Program indicate to the contrary that the police do not appreciate the extent to which citizens feel the need to turn to them for aid and assistance. Notwithstanding, however, it is all too obvious that there is often considerable hostility from the community when peacekeeping and community-service functions are being carried out—and this negative response hardly encourages superior community-service performance.

One successful and high-ranking officer with whom I talked stated that community service had been a major motivation for his applying to the police department, but that a few years later he had been glad to get off patrol. "You can't do anything for people who don't respond with at least a little gratitude," he remarked, citing instances where he had tried to be helpful to people in the community only to be rebuffed and regarded as an enemy. One policeman said he had been called in an emergency to see a woman who was in labor. He delivered her baby

*Throughout this chapter the term "supervisory" refers to middle-management personnel in direct supervisory relationship to the patrolman. In Miami, this is roughly equivalent to ranks of sergeant through captain. "Command" refers to members of the department with over-all decision making responsibility and indirect supervisory control. In Miami, this roughly corresponds to ranks of major through chief.

26

on the spot—this was a ghetto neighborhood and he was white—and on leaving the apartment house he was pelted with bricks from neighbors.*

Hostile reaction is not confined to the black community. For example, the police chief had assigned a specific community service task to his patrolmen. Each was to make brief verbal contact with one citizen every day simply to establish police presence in a friendly and positive way. Some of the policemen were bitter about this. A typical statement was, "When I went into a store to establish my contact, the owner was rude and wanted me out of there as fast as possible; cops spell trouble, and the same bastard who wants me available in thirty seconds when he is robbed throws me the hell out when I'm just trying to be friendly." Because they are so unpleasant and so frequent, such incidents linger on in the mind of the policeman longer than his experiences of cooperation on the part of the citizenry.

Equally frustrating to the police in their roles as peacekeepers and community service agents is the insecurity which community service calls generate. Policemen are untrained to intervene effectively in family fights; they have no medical background; they have few links with the medical, welfare, and social-service resources in the community; and they have no real power to act (short of arrest) in many citizen disputes. Therefore, when asked to perform a community service (often at night or on weekends when other resources are not available), they feel unable to do it properly.

*Stories such as this abound in the department, and one might be tempted to ascribe them to police bigotry. However, if time is spent riding with policemen it can be observed that incidents like this are common. For example, on one call, the police were asked to quiet a noisy, drunken party that was causing a disturbance. When they arrived—again, white policemen in a black neighborhood—a black woman opened the door. It appeared to the gathering crowd as if there were a confrontation developing between a white policeman and a black woman, when in fact the policeman was simply serving the peacekeeping interests of the neighborhood. The crowd became angry; the observer perceived enormous hostility and possible danger to the policeman and himself.

Police leave community-service and peacekeeping calls with no sense of having solved, ended, or "closed out" a problem. This commonly happens when they are called into a citizen dispute—family fights, tenant-landlord squabbles, even fare disputes between taxi drivers and passengers. The police have no real power to settle any of these except by arrest, which is almost always inappropriate. The best they can do is try (often unsuccessfully) to calm the participants down and then leave. After many such calls, the police are left with the feeling that they have accomplished little or nothing, and that they have wasted their time. Patrolmen contrast the frustration experienced after such calls with the "best" type of call in which the police apprehend a felon during an illegal act, arrest him, book him, and put him in jail. This "best" call has a beginning, a middle, and an end and feels like a good job well done.

Frustration with the peacekeeping and community-service roles leads the policeman to be angry with the community he serves—particularly with the black community that calls on him for much of this service. The policeman begins to develop stereotypes that reinforce any preexisting prejudiced attitudes he has. The officer's peers who have been through the same frustrations, support his tendency to stereotype the citizenry as the "bad guys" and tend to acculturate the young policeman in simplistic thinking about the complexities of the urban scene. Since we observed that this peer-group influence is more important to the patrolman than the attitudes of his supervisors or commanders, the young officer will come to regard peacekeeping and community service as unimportant, unrewarding, frustrating, and not part of real policing.

The Boredom of Patrolling

That aspect of the peacekeeping role causing particular problems is preventive patrol. In terms of time spent, the most substantial job of police patrol in Miami is simply to be the visible

28

presence of the government—a sort of human scarecrow to keep crime and disorder away. The police believe very firmly, and probably with good reason, that their patrolling presence is a powerful peacekeeping and crime-deterring force. When policemen of all ranks and years of experience were asked about the usefulness of patrol, the answers were usually along the line of "Who's going to start trouble with a police car coming down the street?" or, "We put the fear of God into them," or "They're searching their souls when we're riding around."

In Miami, much of the time is taken up simply in cruising over and over again through an assigned zone of the city. Our study shows that the average number of police-citizen contacts on an eight-hour shift is 4.4. Though we did not time the duration of contacts, it is unlikely that they averaged an hour each; but even if they did average an hour, then 3.6 hours of each eight-hour shift (about 43 per cent of the time) is taken up with simply cruising. That is a conservative estimate.

As a result, the patrolman, particularly at night, is subjected to severe boredom and lack of sensory stimulation. Policemen have a number of ways of coping with this. Some of them periodically get out of their assigned zone and race along for a few minutes on a superhighway. Some, I have been told (but for obvious reasons did not observe), look for women and engage in sexual intercourse. Some sleep. If one isn't in a two-man car with a partner to talk to, other more common devices for combatting boredom are stopping to chat with other patrolmen or backing up a neighboring patrol car sent on a call. Some policemen endeavor to "look for action" by self-initiated police-citizen contacts and investigations. In our study, the frequency of police-citizen contacts initiated by patrolmen was at its peak from two to four a.m., when boredom and sensory deprivation were at their most intense. (In the ghetto, however, self-initiated contacts generally are avoided, at least by white policemen, because the citizens are feared and the streets are viewed as dangerous and hostile.)

When these devices have all been exhausted, the policeman still spends a good deal of his time simply riding around, scanning the same city blocks hour after hour and day after day. Many policemen spoke of how tiring and enervating this experience is. After a dull night patrol, policemen reported severe fatigue and insomnia.

Under these conditions, psychological regression is apt to take place.* Heron cites a study done by Hebb in which students subjected to sensory deprivation develop fears of ghosts, irritability, inability to control the contents of their minds, childish behavior, mood swings, and at times, hallucinations.[29] The findings of John Zubek and his associates are similar, and he also noted a tendency in his subjects to brooding and dwelling on imaginary injustices.[30] Because of these same effects, the boredom encountered on preventive patrol has an important effect on the outcome of the identity crisis of the policeman. We have seen how his tendencies toward the community-service and peacekeeping roles have been frustrated by other factors; boredom meanwhile heightens his tendencies to suspicion and cynicism. Periods of fantasy engaged in during boring, uneventful patrols sensitize the policeman to the prejudices preached by some of his peers and supervisors. The negative interchanges between himself and minority-group citizens (and by the nature of his work most of his interchanges are negative) are mulled over again and again while he rides around with nothing else to do. He may begin, like Hebb's subjects, to fear ghosts, but his ghosts are black. He loses some of his intellectual capacity to discriminate between those black citizens who turn to him for assistance and protection and those who flaunt his authority and break the law. He becomes more susceptible to the view

---

*Recent studies by Philip Solomon and Susan T. Kleeman have emphasized the difficulties of interpreting findings in conditions of sensory deprivation.[28] The ideas that follow should therefore be read as questions raised rather than as final answers given.

that blacks are "the cause of 99 per cent of the crime around here."*

Thus, fantasy, amplification of paranoid thoughts, and stereotyping during patrol lead to further downgrading of the peace-keeping and community-service aspects of policing and to increased need for the action and stimulus of crime fighting. This is not to suggest that boredom is the sole or even sufficient explanation for police prejudice. Still, our observations indicate that the boredom of patrol is one important factor in the shaping of the young patrolman's identity.

The type of supervisory personnel with whom the police officer comes in contact will also be of great importance. Those who have successfully shaped their own professional identities will help the recruit do the same; those who settle their own identity conflicts poorly will have the opposite influence. I observed one situation in which a senior officer's cool manner in dispersing a crowd clearly served as a role model for his young partner, who began imitating this behavior. In contrast, an experienced officer who repeatedly provoked citizens into quarrels influenced his rookie partner to do the same.

The upper levels of command have less influence on the behavior of the patrolman on the street than his peer group and immediate supervisors. Command in Miami holds a balanced view between the law-enforcement, order-maintenance, and community-service functions of the police, taking the position that each is essential to the other and emphasizing discipline, professionalism, and the importance of centralized command. This is a somewhat complex philosophy, and furthermore its source is so remote that the patrolman finds difficulty in identifying with it in his struggle to master his role conflicts.

---

*In Miami, the situation is heightened by the presence of the Cuban minority. Cubans represent about 30 per cent of the population of Miami. They are seen by the police as good, law-abiding, respectful, and industrious; this serves further to heighten the police stereotype of the black community as the reverse of all of these things.

jesse rubin

The Lure of Crime Fighting

Eventually—usually within a year—the crime-fighting role becomes central to the policeman's view of his work. The apprehension of the felon becomes a major source of gratification and excitement to the policeman. William A. Westley observes that "the apprehension and conviction of the felon is, for the policeman, the essence of police work. It is the source of prestige both within and without police circles. It has career implications and it is a major source of justification for the existence of the police before a critical and often hostile public . . . . The 'good pinch' is elevated to a major end in the conduct of the policeman."[31]

The need to fill the crime-fighter role can be carried to great lengths. A burglary-in-progress call on the radio will draw large numbers of patrol cars in addition to those directly ordered to the scene. The police come partly to help, but also partly to participate in a "good pinch." One night, I rode with a police officer who was becoming more and more restless as the uneventful night wore on. Near the end of the shift, a clearly drunken man raised his hand to hail us; I was sure he mistook the police car for a taxi cab. The officer in the patrol car jumped out, grabbed the man, and told him he was going to arrest him. When the man protested, the officer threw him roughly in the back seat, got into the car, and explained to me that the man had made a threatening and obscene gesture at him and was guilty of public drunkenness and resisting arrest. The policeman was excited and satisfied by his "crime-fighting" activity. He needed to get it out of his system before the end of his tour of duty. On another occasion a woman complained of a purse-snatching. The two policemen involved repeatedly prodded her to say that she had offered physical resistance and had been assaulted during the commission of this crime. When asked why they had done this, they replied that if there were physical combat, the crime would be elevated to the status of a robbery. Their pursuit of the criminal thus would be more exciting and more important.

But even the coveted crime-fighter role is filled with frustration and disappointment for the policeman. He may think of himself primarily as a crime fighter, but he does little of it, and he views that little as relatively ineffective. The patrolman can be active only in the apprehension of the criminal during the act. If a felony has already been committed, all he can do is take statements of victims and witnesses. The felon is later apprehended, if at all, by the detective division. And if a policeman *does* catch a felon, he feels hamstrung in the pursuit, apprehension, and jailing of the criminal by recent civil-rights decisions of the courts. Later it may be that he feels further frustrated by postponement, leniency, or acquittal at trial.

A specific function of the crime-fighting role—record-keeping—is particularly onerous. On the one hand, the police believe that by keeping meticulous records, the department builds up enough data to apprehend more criminals. On the other hand, policemen are not adept at record-keeping. It is a difficult and fatiguing task for them. Our statistics show that the greatest switch in categories of calls from precall signal to final signal was made *into* those categories that require no reports to be written. Watson found that "too much paper work" ranked first among job problems for policemen.[32]

Individual Versus Team Player

Another conflict for the policeman arises from being part of a paramilitary and authoritarian organization. He carries a weapon, wears a uniform, and advances with military rank (sergeant, lieutenant, etc.). This implies that policing involves commitment to a chain of command, submission to authority, and capacity to function as part of a well-disciplined team. The reality is that policemen have a highly ambivalent attitude toward command and authority, because the military role conflicts with another, antimilitary, police identity—the policeman's identification with the gunslinging marshall of the Old

West, maintaining law and order in his own territory, alone and unassisted. In further contrast to the military, where the commitment of major forces can only be made by command, a single patrolman acting alone can commit an entire police force to an action before the chief knows what has happened.[33]

The conflict between the individualistic, gunslinging marshall and the group or team player is understandable. The patrolman must be intimately familiar with his particular zone of the city so that he can scan the environment for minor changes that indicate trouble. Police work also requires that rapid decisions be made in the field without constant reference to supervisors through the radio. In such a situation, it becomes difficult to distinguish useful autonomy from unwillingness to accept discipline. "When we're out there, we're on our own," patrolmen often say, or "no one else understands or knows what's going on." Or "every situation is separate and different." In line with this, Watson found that only 50 per cent of policemen agreed with the statement, "The good policeman is one who gives his commanding officer unquestioning obedience."[34]

When I was riding with patrolmen, they were often resentful when word came via the radio that the sector supervisor was on his way. This attitude was most prevalent in the patrol section. In the tactical squad, which is more concerned with apprehension of felons and is not anchored geographically to a particular sector of the city, discipline and submission to command were more apparent and less ambivalent.

Thus far I have discussed authority in terms of the patrolman and supervisory personnel, but the feeling about command's authority is also ambivalent. Some Miami patrolmen idealized the previous police chief who would "back up his men no matter what they did." Translated, that meant he would not discipline them. Under that kind of regime, the department had encouraged the lone-gunslinger identity of its men. In contrast, the current police chief has made it clear that his men would

34

need to be more responsive to command than they ever had been in the past. Many patrolmen have not accepted this.

Despite the policeman's ambivalence, more sophisticated communications and computer systems will inevitably bring command closer to the man on the street. For example, when I first began working with the Miami police, radios in patrol cars had just been augmented by individually carried radios. This meant that at no time would a patrolman be out of touch with the station. Though this did not immediately bring the men under tighter command influence, such an outcome is only a matter of time. In addition, computer analysis of patterns of criminal activity will result in more centralized, higher-level decisions about where men are to be deployed and for what specific purposes.* This is hardly an atmosphere congenial to a lone gunslinger.

The Quasi-Judicial Role of the Policeman

Policemen cannot enforce all the laws all the time even if they tried, nor does anyone really expect them to do so.[35] However, there exists no social consensus about which laws to enforce, against which violators, and under what conditions. Prominent examples are laws concerning gambling, alcoholism, drug use, adult sexual behavior, and minor traffic offenses. There is also no clear understanding about how much discretion policemen should (or do) have.

The Miami police see the misdemeanor laws as their main discretionary lever. Misdemeanors are not viewed by the police as real breaches of the law, to be enforced as such. Rather, the police see misdemeanor violations as giving them enough discretion to investigate citizens whom they feel are suspicious. Policemen call this "checking someone out." Over and over

---

*It should be noted also that the policeman is required increasingly to respond to civil disorders, which are best handled when police operate as a well-disciplined team responsive to tight control.

35

again I heard the remark, "If you follow anybody for three minutes, he's going to break some kind of law, and then you can check him out." Examples of this were legion. One officer stopped a car going just a few miles over the limit, not because it was speeding, but because he suspected it might be stolen. Another followed a car for minor speeding because it contained two white girls driving through a black neighborhood, and the officer wondered whether they were involved in prostitution or drug traffic. Another asked women in a bar for identification, ostensibly to make sure they were of age, but actually so that he could run a radio check on them for prostitution or other illegal activities.

Warning citizens about breaches of misdemeanor laws are also viewed by the police as a method of maintaining order because somebody who has been so warned will "have the fear of God in him" when he thinks about committing a felony.

This discretionary role, however, has not been explicitly sanctioned by society (nor even by command within the department). Since the police lack guidelines for the exercise of their discretionary function, citizens question the criteria on which they do exercise it. Citizens stopped for checking out purposes complain of harrassment and feel that skin color, quality of clothes, make of car, and "respectability"—i.e., social class— rather than wrongdoing, determine whether a citizen will attract the attention of the police. Once again, the policeman is in a bind, and the bind relates to an essential component of his role. He is expected to function in a discretionary, quasi-judicial role, but this role is not even ill-defined—it is not defined at all.

The Police and the Establishment

Finally, the police role with regard to the established order is unclear. Are policemen the disinterested enforcement arm of an impartial judicial system? Or is the police function, as suggested by Joseph Lowman, "to support and enforce the interest of the dominant, political, social, and economic interests of the town, and only incidentally to enforce the law?"[36] One policeman with whom I rode was instructed to drive through a walled, barricaded, and guarded area, one of the wealthiest neighborhoods in town, twice during each of his patrols. This seemed unnecessary—he had never seen or heard of a disturbance there—but it protected the established order from intruders. We observed differences in police behavior toward poor people and blacks compared to their attitude toward white and upper-class citizens. This suggests that one role that they often fill is the protection of the established order, though this conflicts with the stated ideal of professionalism and impartiality.

The Conflicts of the Black Policeman

Our study thus far indicates that the personality of the black man who is attracted to police work cannot be differentiated from that of the white. Disdain for routine or an indoor job and a thirst for action, for example, are characteristics shared by both black and white officers. It is obvious, however, that the black policeman has certain unique role conflicts and consequent identity problems. If one assumes that the police and the ghetto are at war, then the black policeman has an unsolvable identity conflict which can be summed up in a single question: "When the chips are down, what is he—a cop or a black?"

The point has been made many times and in various ways as, for example, in this statement by a policeman in a letter to *The New York Times:* "Recently when two policemen were brutally murdered in New York, a description of two black perpetrators went out over the police radio. A voice, obviously that of a white policeman, bitterly cut in, advising the killing of 'all the black so-and-so's.' Later regret for this hasty invective could not wipe out the animosity created, and the disclosure that one of the murdered men was black ironically shows *the ambiguous position of the black policeman of today*." (Italics added.)[37] Or take a recent *Newsweek* article that quotes two policemen: "The problem in the black community is the feeling that once a

37

black becomes a cop he's become a traitor to them . . . . They
think we're only interested in carrying out the wishes of the
white Establishment," and "I wouldn't work in Harlem . . .
because I just can't take the way I'd have to treat my
brothers."[38]

To be sure, similar problems were found in Miami. For example, a black officer said that black citizens sometimes express
their hatred for black officers by resisting arrests made by
blacks, but then go along submissively when a white officer is
called to help.

But perhaps too much emphasis has been put on the stresses
and strains imposed on the black policeman by being the man in
the middle, and not enough on the positive and useful functions
he can serve. The "war" theory of police-ghetto relations, as
James Q. Wilson points out in the following chapter, is at best a
gross distortion and oversimplification. By and large, most community residents not only support police work, but want more
police protection. Community residents participating in the
Miami Police-Community Interaction Project reported a good
deal of concern for the quality and quantity of police work in
their neighborhood and consistently asked for better police protection. When a recent bond issue for better communications,
computer systems, and physical facilities for the Miami police
was proposed, as many as 90 per cent of the voters in some
model-city ghetto precincts voted for the issue, as contrasted
with 58.7 per cent of the Miami population at large.[39]

If one assumes that the police department as a *whole* and the
ghetto as a *whole* are not in fact at war, but rather that they
share many common problems, then there can be important and
positive aspects to the black policeman's role as the man in the
middle. Though black policemen's view of black crime-ridden
areas is as negative as that of white officers, they do not ascribe
this to racial or genetic factors.[40] They are therefore more able
to maintain their self-image as peacekeepers and community-

service agents and to find that image confirmed and reflected in the black community. It is unquestionably true that black officers move more comfortably in ghetto areas in Miami than white officers do.

Our most striking finding, however, was that those black officers who knew the neighborhood were even markedly more at ease and accepted than were their black fellow officers from outside the neighborhood. The fact of being indigenous could almost be said to be more important than the color of the officer's skin. For example, a racially mixed group of policemen apprehended an armed man wanted for a felony offense. The man was caught on a busy ghetto street. As a crowd began to form, both the black and white officers who were unfamiliar with the neighborhood became apprehensive. The most junior of the policemen, a rookie with only about six months on the force, had grown up in the neighborhood. He spoke in a bantering fashion with the people gathering, and his light tone and sense of familiarity with the crowd kept a potentially explosive situation cool.

In the Miami Police-Community Interaction Project, we found that black officers were sensitive to issues raised indirectly by both the white policemen and the black community residents, and aggressively brought these issues to the fore when the other participants tended to skirt around them.[41]

If the black policeman sees himself as *passively* caught between a black community that regards him as a sellout and a white establishment police organization that does not fully accept him (the *Newsweek* perspective), his role conflict will be severe indeed, and will lead to bitterness, rage and defeatism. Our observations indicated, however, that if he is able to see himself as a professional policeman, who can effect changes on both sides of the police-black conflict by being an *active* mediator, he will gain an inner sense of strength through conflict resolution.

39

jesse rubin

Recommendations

Thus far we have applied Erikson's theory of identity formation to the young police officer by examining the interaction of his personality with his job, and we have seen how his expectations may be frustrated by his work experience. As a result, some young policemen settle into a work identity characterized by disrespect for citizenry, an emphasis on crime fighting to the detriment of peacekeeping and community service, disregard for discipline and command, and poor use of discretionary powers. Most tragically, stress and role conflict lead to a sacrifice of that potential for continuous growth which is a hallmark of the true professional, making it difficult for the policeman to adapt to the changing demands on him from an increasingly complex and crime-ridden urban society. One command-level officer said that contemporary police work was "like working for a guy who keeps changing the rules all the time." Officers who settle into a rigid behavioral pattern cannot cope with these changing rules in a professional manner.

The recommendations that follow are directed to ways of helping the police officer achieve a professional identity by clarifying and simplifying his role. Sidney Epstein states the problem succinctly:

The key fact affecting the place of applied behavioral research in police work today is *the rapidly changing nature of the police role itself.* Because the police role is changing, all other aspects of police personnel will have to change, including selection methods and training and education practices. If this important commonplace is overlooked, there is little chance of advancing beyond the trouble-shooting mode in police research and development work . . . *role research is not simply a matter of summing up, tidying up, and systematizing present day practice. It is also a matter of modifying, adding to, and subtracting from present day practice.* (Italics added.)[42]

If police roles can be clarified, simplified and specialized, men can be recruited and trained specifically for each role. The

40

policeman will then have a better chance of shaping his emerging identity to fit *realizable* role expectations, *limited* in number. As his specific role becomes clearer to the community, a better congruence of self-concept and reflected image should emerge.

Following work done on an experimental basis in Great Britain and the United States since World War II, Bernard L. Garmire has proposed long-range changes in police strategy aimed at clarifying role expectations for each policeman. The following remarks explore the potential effect of these proposals, which are described in the previous chapter. Perhaps the most fundamental role conflict described is that between the peacekeeping, community service, and order-maintenance roles on the one hand, and the crime-fighting role on the other.

A Community Service Arm. Order-maintenance, peacekeeping, community-service, and some crime-fighting functions all derive naturally from a single agreed-upon police role—that of crime prevention. Community service leads to crime prevention indirectly though powerfully. Insofar as policemen aid the sick or are of real help in settling family disputes, they build up a community conception of them as a benign but forceful presence and gain friends in the community who can be useful in crime-prevention activities (or who at least will not obstruct these activities). Policemen who are known in a neighborhood through peacekeeping and community service activities are in a better position to prevent crime than those who are viewed by the neighborhood as a member of an army of occupation and who in turn see the streets as alien, unknown, hostile territory bristling with snipers. The development of a section of the force whose role is defined primarily as crime prevention (via peacekeeping and community service) will help delineate role expectation for police officers whose jobs are so defined.

The Neighborhood Police Team. Further evolution of the concept of the community-service (or crime-deterrent) police arm led to the notion of the neighborhood policing team.

Under the team-policing concept, a group of patrolmen serve peacekeeping, order-maintenance, and possibly auxiliary-patrol functions such as traffic control and investigation in an assigned neighborhood. Each officer is expected to become intimately familiar with the entire territory covered by the team. Members of such a team see themselves as community-service and peacekeeping personnel, these functions deriving from the primary mission, that of crime prevention. Such a team also functions in criminal apprehension on routine cases but can call on the "crimefighting" policemen for more difficult, complex, or unusual police operations. (Their functions are described in the next section.) Particular sectors or zones of the neighborhood do not "belong" to any particular patrolman. He is part of the team and subject to the discipline and group feeling that that involves.

Men could be selected and trained to be compatible with this view of police operations, and their performance could be evaluated consistent with this. A neighborhood police team, with this explicit mission, would go a long way toward solving the identity and role conflict experienced by patrolmen. The members of such a team would see their role clearly, and rewards would come from excellence in this role.

The neighborhood police team will function best when each patrolman is a "generalist-specialist." That is, each member of the team policing a neighborhood should be trained both as a neighborhood patrolman-generalist and also as a specialist in a particular peacekeeping or community-service aspect of police work. Morton Bard describes policemen trained in family-crisis intervention work.[43] But other generalist-specialists could be trained to work with youth in the schools, to function as paramedical personnel (particularly in dealing with acute alcoholics and drug addicts), or to be community organization specialists. Each of these must first and foremost be a police officer and second a specialist. In the training of the generalist-specialist, Bard states, "If there is a single most significant factor in its approach, it is that *role identity confusion in the officers was avoided.* Throughout the project, every effort was made to avoid giving the men the notion that they were functioning in any other way than as police officers. *Their professional identities were respected and preserved and, indeed, constantly reinforced.*" (Italics added.)[44]

Under the current system, each police officer is expected to perform all police roles expertly, but he is poorly prepared for most and implicitly disavows some. Combining the generalist-specialist model with the neighborhood police-team concept, the number of roles would be cut down considerably and the expertise with which each patrolman could function within his defined roles would be increased. Also, training each policeman in a specialty would give him more to do in the neighborhood and would thus alleviate the harmful effects of boredom.

The Crime Fighters. The second arm of the police would be a target- and crime-oriented force composed of men specifically recruited, trained, and deployed for *crime-fighting activities*; it would be mobile and flexible rather than neighborhood based. It would move against crime—particularly street crime and violent crime—where and when it occurs. It would serve also as the basic unit to respond to large emergency operations, civil disturbances, and acts of urban terrorism. Where the patrol officer could not cope with a situation, the tactical crime-fighting officer would back him up.[45]

The potential of such units to curb and prevent crime will increase as departments develop more sophisticated information systems to enable them to react more and more quickly to developing patterns of criminal activity. Eventually, it may even be possible to anticipate such activity rather than simply respond to it.[46]

Thus, the crime-fighting arm would also have its role clearly defined. Men could be recruited, trained, and deployed in ways consistent with this role.

From the model of policing presented, there follows a diminution of the conflict between the gunslinger and the organization man. Communication and information systems will inevitably make the policemen in both arms less independent of command. The team-policing concept would diminish the "territoriality" of the individual policeman. His need to work in tandem with other generalist-specialists on a number of police calls would engender more cooperation with other members of the department. As a result, the gunslinger role would diminish considerably in favor of an organizational approach, with the men more responsive to command.

Recruitment. What sort of man brings to police service a personality structure most conducive to the development of a professional work identity? To a large extent, we do not know. We can only make some educated guesses.

Given the complexities of police work, it would seem self-evident that the more highly intelligent men one can recruit, the better. This common sense point of view has seemingly been challenged by William H. Thweatt's study of the Tucson police department, which revealed that the IQ scores of policemen who dropped out of the force were "significantly higher" than the norm group. "Does this mean one can be too bright to be a cop?" Thweatt asks, and replies to his own question with a vitally important qualification: "Yes, *unless an alternate career-development program can be developed to challenge and use these bright men.*" (Italics added.)[47]

In terms of psychological factors, Melany E. Baehr's work indicates that certain traits are important to good police performance. It is important that "they [policemen] assume family responsibility early, by establishing a family and a home, and that they evidence some stability both in their family and in their occupational environments."[48] Baehr goes on to say,

The desirable response is one of cooperation and active endeavor to solve the problem rather than withdrawal from the situation, undue competitiveness in attempting to resolve it by outdoing others, or an expression of hostility toward it... [Other] desirable attributes are those which make for control of purely impulsive and emotional responses and for a "work"

44

rather than a "social" orientation . . . personal confidence, resistance to stress, and a realistic rather than a subjective and feeling-oriented approach to life.[49]

As a yardstick of performance, the Baehr study used the judgment of policemen's superiors and did not attempt to measure successful performance in different police roles. Nonetheless, it constitutes an important effort in the development of standardized psychological tests to predict police performance.

On the basis of our own early findings, there is no evidence that simple paper and pencil tests can adequately differentiate those who can perform well in any of the police roles. Policemen who seem to have a proven record of success in police work, as now constituted, have the same *qualitative* personality structures as those who precipitate unnecessary police-citizen problems and cause trouble for the community and the department. The differences between good and bad officers are *quantitative*. The good policeman is suspicious, aggressive, and restless. In the poor policeman, suspicion becomes paranoia, restlessness becomes a need to harass, and aggression becomes sadism. Therefore, it would seem sensible that overwhelming predispositions to paranoia, sadism, or indeed any other severe degree of psychiatric disability would make a cadet a poor risk.

Careful screening can help weed out those who are most apt to be disturbed and impulsive. However, the best tool that we have for such screening at the moment is the good clinical judgment of a psychiatrist supported by extensive psychological testing. Clinical judgment, however, is rare, expensive, and—at times—inaccurate. We need badly to develop more precise instruments for prediction of performance which are cheaply and readily available to police departments; however, it will take several years and much more research before such instruments are reliably developed.

In terms of viewing selection positively (that is, selecting *in* the best men as opposed to weeding *out* the worst), this cannot be done at present. Until a clarification and restructuring of police roles is accomplished, I believe such a task will remain impossible.

Should the model of policing presented above be implemented, the selection problem offers the exciting possibility of becoming at once more complex and more hopeful. Once roles are clarified, it should be possible to look for men who could optimally function as neighborhood team members or as crime fighters; ideally some men even may be found who could do either. At the moment, we have absolutely no basis on which to select accurately such men. This is a task for the future—but if we have some conception of what we are recruiting *for*, selection techniques can certainly be developed.

Training and Professionalism. Insofar as training is inadequate or irrelevant to a man when he gets on the street, the exercise of any of the defined police roles on the street becomes an art, heavily dependent on acculturation to the peer group, identification with older policemen, and the development of an individual style. As with any art form, born artists are rare in police work. Because of the pressures which we have discussed above, there are a number of factors militating against the policeman-artist in the streets functioning within the ideal of police professionalism. The situation in our cities will no longer permit us the luxury of hoping for policemen-artists to come along.

Yet policing will never become a science in the sense of having closely and logically set rules governing each situation, in which the predictability of outcome is very high. Even given the trends regarding centralization of discipline and command, it is difficult to envision a time when set rules, rationally derived, will dictate a policeman's behavior in all possible situations on the street. Human interactions and human beings being what they are, the degree of uncertainty about any police-citizen encounter will remain fairly high. However, if our earlier definitions of professionalism are to be a guide, then police training

46

must be rigorous and must inculcate basic and practical principles to govern the policeman's behavior. Once he has mastered these, he can exercise his judgment against a background of educational and organizational discipline.

In order to accomplish this goal, academy training should prepare police for their specific roles. Certain learning techniques would be of use in this regard. Two of these are group techniques and semiprogrammed learning techniques.

Group methods which would be useful in police training include: (1) classroom discussions concerning police roles in which the functions of each arm of the police department and of each generalist-specialist are made clear; (2) lectures from successful "role models" imparting guidelines for the types of peacekeeping, community-service, and crime-fighting behavior expected, and explicitly outlining the departmental rewards to be used; (3) action (psychodramatic) methods, films depicting street situations coupled with post-film discussions, and street re-creation (simulation) of difficult situations. Such training techniques can be taught by professionals in group work to police training officers.

Another learning technique, that of self-paced, semiprogrammed instruction, can save time in training programs. This time could be devoted to the practical preparation for police work, an apprenticeship in the field, or teaching officers to make their report writing an easier skill.

The Acculturation Process. The influences on the acculturation to the department of the new policeman are, in descending order, his peer group, his supervisors, and command. Peer-group pressures toward a productive resolution of the identity crisis can be accomplished only by gradually instilling a clear understanding of the roles that the new recruit's peers are to perform, the value placed on each role by command, and the shaping of the group's behavior to conform with the roles most highly valued by command through specifically built-in rewards. Men so trained would in turn acculturate the new recruit. Through team policing and improved communications, a reordered priority of influence on the recruit may be achieved. That is, he may become more susceptible to the influence of command than to that of his peer group. Since command personnel represent the best of policing, the young policeman will be able to utilize the earliest and most effective means of achieving a positive identity, i.e., identification with the parent figure. Certain things must be accomplished to do this. First, command must convey a clear idea of the roles which it wishes its policemen to fill. This is difficult to do amidst the inevitable pressures from within the department, from government, from the media, and from the community at large. Second, those in command must themselves provide models of professionalism with which the cadet can identify.

Police-Community Relations. Recommendations in this area concern, first, police-community relations programs, and, second, the development of generalist-specialists in community relations.

Our experience indicates that through well-designed and implemented programs, police and community members can productively work together to reduce stereotypes and to obtain realistic and individualized pictures of each other. But if police-community relations programs are to be useful, certain basic elements must be built into them.

(1) They must have the complete confidence and backing of the police chief. (The Interaction program in Miami at times produced external political pressures and internal departmental conflict. The backing of the chief was absolutely essential to its success.)

(2) The programs must be long enough so that initial hostilities can be worked through between police and community residents and *specific productive work* done. In Miami, each group of policemen and community members worked together full time for two weeks. I would consider this an absolute mini-

48

mum. The resultant drain on police manpower must be antici-
pated and planned for.

(3) Directors of programs must be carefully chosen and have
an extensive background in the conduct of task-oriented groups.

(4) Staff members must also be carefully chosen and well
trained. The use of unqualified personnel in these positions
leads to useless rancor among program participants without resolution of problems. Staff must include community organizers,
police officers, and group leaders, as well as support staff.

(5) Programs must be task oriented, having as their prime
focus not simply the ventilation of feeling, but the accomplishment of certain specific tasks. Tasks should be self-determined
but should relate to problems of mutual concern to police and
residents.

(6) Funding must be sufficient to allow follow through on
specific projects generated by the program. In Miami, for example, these projects included establishment of a police-
community liaison board; endeavors to improve recreational
facilities within the neighborhood; a project to get school dropouts back to school and to maintain them in school; confer-
ences between residents and the police chief; arrangements for
K-9 Corps demonstrations; and streamlining of telephone communication between the community and the department.

The development of a cadre of generalist-specialist policemen
who would function as community organizers as well as be
members of police teams offers another possibility of improving
police-community relations. Such a generalist-specialist would
be specially recruited and trained in community liaison. He
would attempt basically to recreate the original function of the
police—to organize and supervise the citizenry for peacekeeping
purposes.* He would establish contact with community leaders,

*The seeds of such a program were sown in the Miami Police-Community
Interaction Program. A number of citizens publicly stated that they
wanted to cooperate with the police, again in contrast to the "war" theory
of police-community relations.

school personnel, concerned parents, church groups and other centers of community concern, and maintain a cooperative relationship with them. This approach seems to me more useful than assigning a policeman to an isolated community relations section where he is not able fully to assume a police identity and is not considered a "real policeman" by the rest of the force. (The community relations section is referred to by some members in the police department in Miami as "the rubber gun police," though it is staffed by highly professional officers.)

In conclusion, let me reiterate a point made several times in this chapter. The ideas presented here are tentative. Collaboration between police and behavioral scientists is in its early stages. Research in this area is inherently difficult. As Epstein points out,

The critical thing to remember about a police department as a setting for research is that its tolerance for serving in this capacity is limited. It is possible to saturate the police community with research in such a way as either to build up an inhibition or resistance to further research, or to damage the usefulness or suitability of many departments for some or all kinds of behavioral research in the future. If a researcher antagonizes the police, gets under foot too much, is indiscreet, interferes with operations, or otherwise "leaves a bad taste in their collective mouths" he will wear out his welcome very fast . . . . Disruption of police operations for purposes of research is unacceptable.[50]

Major funding sources such as the U.S. Department of Justice and the Police Foundation, endowed by The Ford Foundation, have served to focus the public's eye on the need for further research in this area. How badly that is needed is perceived most acutely by those working actively in the field.

3 the police in the ghetto
james q. wilson

Increasingly, public accounts of the relations between the police
and the big-city ghettoes are portrayed in the language of war.
In black areas where residents are seething with resentment and
hostility, the police are an "army of occupation"; any incident
may touch off armed conflict and rioting; attitudes are so polar-
ized as to prevent any agreement on what standards of justice or
order ought to prevail; only luck or superior force keeps the
subject population from waging a constant guerilla struggle
against the police. Among the phrases that make the headlines
are cries of "get the pigs" aimed by young black militants at
police; the scenes that dominate television show club-swinging
officers wading into groups of students or blacks; the spokesmen who get attention are those who most frequently and
vividly predict Armageddon. As a background to the angry talk
and violent encounters, the crime rates mount steadily, especially those for street crimes. We seem to have entered into a
Hobbesian state of nature, a war of all against all, in which—
unless the situation is dramatically reversed—life for the urban

citizen will soon become "solitary, poor, nasty, brutish, and short."

It is not hard to find evidence for this view. In the first eight months of 1970, fifteen patrolmen were killed by unprovoked attacks, double the number thus killed in the whole of 1969 and triple the average for the last ten years.[1] In turn, there have been police raids on buildings thought to be harboring snipers, with innocent people caught in the middle. Police officers killed a Black Panther in a Chicago raid under circumstances that have led many to conclude they shot first and asked questions later. Newspaper headlines frequently have stated that twenty-eight Panthers have been killed by the police. The president of Yale University has publicly expressed doubts about the ability of a militant black to receive justice in parts of this country. Police precinct stations and patrol cars have been bombed. As the tension mounts, officers in some cities tend to ignore certain infractions, to respond cautiously rather than quickly to calls for assistance, and to avoid speaking with residents of black areas. As one Detroit officer put it, "Get in and get out as fast as possible."

If indeed a state of war exists between the police and the ghettos, there is little point in considering whether to adopt the kinds of remedies that are at our disposal. One cannot ameliorate through government programs a situation in which the legitimacy of government itself is denied. Nor can we imagine ways of improving the police, or altering the attitudes of citizens, if police and citizens alike see each other as implacable enemies, utterly beyond redemption. In the warlike conception of police-ghetto relations, talk of developing community relations programs, experimenting with sensitivity training, finding better qualified officers, and improving communication seem trivial, if not silly.

It is not merely a desire to salvage one's own sense of efficacy, however, that leads one to question the popular account of the police in the ghetto. Perhaps, indeed, the conventional remedies for such problems are trivial. What should give one pause is the awareness that the "war" account purports to describe the attitudes and behavior of millions of people and tens of thousands of police officers living in scores of cities. Generalizing about so many people and so many cities ought not to be undertaken lightly. Furthermore, we should be instinctively chary of relying wholly (if at all) on the media-dramatized views of the police militant and the black militant, for each has a constituency to which he is appealing, a leadership position he is striving to protect, and an awareness of what makes news. Therefore, though the enterprise may seem dull, it is nevertheless important to sift rather carefully such evidence as we have about attitudes of the police and the blacks toward each other and the relations of the two groups. Statistics, though often wearisome, have a way of suggesting the complexity and exceptions that are so often concealed by rhetoric. On this subject, as on so many others, it is necessary to be bored before one can be enlightened.

Citizen Views of the Police

The single most striking fact about the attitudes of citizens, black and white, toward the police is that in general these attitudes are positive, not negative. A study done in 1964 of blacks living in several large cities showed that a majority of those interviewed in Atlanta, Chicago, and New York City thought the police treated blacks "very well" or "fairly well."[2] A study by the National Opinion Research Center (NORC) for the President's Commission on Law Enforcement and the Administration of Justice indicated that among several thousand men, the overwhelming majority of both whites and blacks believed that the police were "very good" or "pretty good" at being respectful to "persons like yourself."[3] A survey of residents of the city of Washington disclosed that among the persons who had reported having recent contact with the police, 78 per cent thought the officer had acted properly.[4] In this study, 80 per cent of the black males said that the police "deserve a lot more respect and thanks than they get."[5] In Hartford, a survey done in 1966 found that 53 per cent of the blacks (compared to 68 per cent of the whites) were satisfied with the way the police were doing their job. When the blacks who reported themselves dissatisfied with the police were asked what would be the best way the police could be improved, the most common answer (given by 34 per cent) was to increase the size of the police force; another 12 per cent called for stricter law enforcement policies. Thus, almost half of those who were dissatisfied wanted more, not less, police presence.[6] In two largely black precincts in Boston and Chicago, only 10 per cent of those citizens interviewed said that they had little or no respect for the way the police did their job.[7] Finally, a survey done for the Kerner Commission indicated that about one-third of the blacks interviewed were critical of the police in their city (believing that the police use insulting language, that they search without reason, and that they rough people up unnecessarily); but not only was this group much less than a majority, it was also about the same size as the group that was critical of the mayor, the state government, the federal government, and local merchants.[8]

Of course, interpreting these findings depends a good deal on how big one thinks a third or a quarter is. With respect to the last study, for example, one could report it either as saying "two-thirds of the blacks were not critical of the police" or as saying "fully [or 'a whopping'] one-third of the blacks were highly critical of the police." Whatever adjectives one chooses to append to these numbers, however, one thing is clear: they offer little support for the view that the great majority of blacks are seething with resentment against the police on grounds of injustice or abuse.

But the over-all figures do not tell the whole story. Contrary to the views of many white racists and black militants, not all blacks are alike. There is a good deal of variation in their attitudes toward the police. All the studies agree on this variation, though not all agree on the source of it. The Boston-Chicago study, for example, finds that black males are more likely than black women to believe that the police treat blacks differently from whites;[9] the Washington study concurs, discovering that just as whites are more "pro-police" than blacks, black women are more pro-police than black men.[10] The NORC study, on the other hand, found black women having the same view of police fairness as black men.[11] The same uncertainty surrounds the roles of income and education. The NORC study found that the more affluent black males were more critical of police fairness (possibly because, being more law-abiding, they were more resentful at being stopped, questioned, or searched);[12] the Washington study, on the other hand, discovered that income made little difference in whether a black was "pro-police."[13] Education also seemed to make little significant difference in black attitudes, at least in Washington and in the Boston-Chicago studies.[14]

The one factor that clearly and powerfully divides the black community in its perception of police behavior is age. In most surveys, only adults are interviewed, and thus the principal source of anti-police attitudes—young males, especially those in minority groups—is not detected. In a study of the Watts area in Los Angeles made shortly after the riot, persons of all ages were questioned about the police (among other things). It found that less than a third (31.4 per cent) of the blacks over the age of forty-five but 60 per cent of those between the ages of fifteen and twenty-nine thought there was some or a great deal of police brutality. Of the males under the age of thirty-five, over half claimed that they had been subjected to insulting language, almost half to a "roust, frisk, or search without good reason," and almost a quarter to "unnecessary force while being arrested."[15]

It is not surprising that young men, whether for good reason or not and especially just after a riot, should dislike the police.

Most crimes, so far as we know, are committed by young men; brawls and rowdiness in which the police must intervene typically involve young males; riot participants tend to be youthful; complaints from citizens about neighborhood nuisances are often directed at the behavior of young men. In any community, black or white, rich or poor, the young man and the police are natural adversaries. The crucial question is whether black young men feel, rightly or wrongly, more aggrieved than their white counterparts. From such evidence as we have, the answer is that they do.

In a study for the Kerner Commission nearly 6,000 persons, black and white, living in fifteen large cities were interviewed. Their attitudes toward and experiences with the police were tabulated by race and age. The results are sufficiently interesting to warrant reporting in full. Tables 1, 2, and 3 show that at all age levels, blacks are more critical of the police than whites—that is, they are much more likely to believe that the police use insulting language, that they frisk and search for no reason, and that they rough people up.[16] In the youngest age group (sixteen to twenty), blacks are twice as likely as whites to have these beliefs, but in the older age groups they are *three or four* times as likely as whites to think this way. Stated another way, a sixty-five-year-old black has the same beliefs about the police as an eighteen-year-old white.

For both blacks and whites, beliefs critical of the police decline in frequency in direct proportion to the age of the person questioned, but the decline is greater for the whites. From age thirty-five on, the great majority of blacks and whites do not have strong anti-police views, but while for the whites criticism is confined to a tiny fraction of the population (about a tenth), for the blacks it remains the active concern of about a quarter or more.

Experience with the police, unlike beliefs about them, follows a somewhat different pattern. In the youngest age group, about twice as many blacks as whites report that they person-

ATTITUDES TOWARD THE POLICE
Based on a Survey of 6,000 Persons,
Black and White, in Fifteen Cities

Table 1: "Police Use Insulting Language"

Age Group (both sexes)	Believe it has happened		Happened to them	
	White	Black	White	Black
16–19	24%	55%	14%	24%
20–29	24	45	11	19
30–39	14	37	7	14
40–49	13	36	3	15
50–59	9	26	6	7
60–69	8	24	3	5

Table 2: "Police Frisk and Search Without Good Reason"

Age Group (both sexes)	Believe it has happened		Happened to them	
	White	Black	White	Black
16–19	25%	51%	12%	22%
20–29	15	43	5	18
30–39	7	33	2	11
40–49	9	32	2	9
50–59	7	28	1	4
60–69	4	24	1	8

Table 3: "Police Rough People Up Unnecessarily"

Age Group (both sexes)	Believe it has happened		Happened to them	
	White	Black	White	Black
16–19	25%	49%	3%	8%
20–29	13	43	1	7
30–39	7	33	3	3
40–49	5	30	0	2
50–59	6	26	1	4
60–69	3	20	0	1

Source: Angus Campbell and Howard Schuman, "Racial Attitudes in Fifteen American Cities," in *Supplemental Studies for the National Advisory Commission on Civil Disorders,* (Washington, D.C.: U.S. Government Printing Office, 1968), p. 44.

ally experienced insulting police language, an unreasonable search, or a roughing up. Past the age of fifty, however, there is not much difference in white and black experience—for both races, only an infinitesimal fraction claim to have been the victims of police malpractice. If this cross section of current black opinion is any guide to how attitudes develop over time (and it may not be), then age does not produce a reconciliation between beliefs and experiences for blacks to the same extent that it does for whites. By the time whites are in their fifties, there are only trivial differences between the proportions reporting an anti-police belief and those reporting an anti-police experience (less than 10 per cent in both cases); at the same age, by contrast, the proportion of blacks with anti-police beliefs (20 to 24 per cent) continues to be larger than that with anti-police experiences (8 per cent or less).

Intensifying anti-police sentiments among young black males is their awareness, in many cities, of police corruption in ghetto neighborhoods. The young male, as an active member of "street society," is often well-informed about local gambling, prostitution, and narcotics enterprises and is thus more likely than older blacks to be alert to signs of police complicity in these rackets. Any claim to moral or legal authority made by a corrupt officer is certain to be greeted with scorn by persons who are aware of the corruption. On the other hand, the relations between young ghetto males and the police is probably as tense and hostile in cities such as Oakland, where police corruption is comparatively rare, as it is in New York, where it is relatively widespread. Out of zeal, an honest officer can produce the same ill will as a dishonest one out of laxity.

It is easy to become preoccupied with criticisms by blacks of alleged police abuse; it is easy to forget that there is as much or more black criticism of inadequate police protection and service. In the Kerner Commission survey, for example, a majority of black respondents believed that the police "don't come quickly" and about a fourth say that this slow response has happened to them. Moreover, these attitudes and experiences, unlike those concerning abuses, do *not* change much with age. About half of all blacks aged twenty to twenty-nine think the police are too slow; about half of those aged sixty to sixty-nine feel the same way. About a quarter of those aged twenty to twenty-nine say they have experienced a slow response; about a quarter of those aged sixty to sixty-nine say the same thing.[17]

The President's Commission on Law Enforcement and the Administration of Justice cited a number of studies showing that in many areas blacks view "crime in the streets" as one of the most important problems afflicting their neighborhood.[18] A study of 300 blacks in thirteen U.S. cities, commissioned by *Fortune* Magazine, indicated that they felt the same way; "better police protection" was the most frequent neighborhood need mentioned (personal concerns, such as better jobs and schooling, had the highest priorities).[19] In December 1968, the New York branch of the National Association for the Advancement of Colored People issued a report demanding a halt to "the reign of criminal terror in Harlem" and called for assigning more police to the area, placing armed guards in housing projects, handing out harsher sentences to those convicted, and disposing more swiftly of criminal cases. The chairman of the branch's anticrime committee told newsmen that "it is not police brutality that makes people afraid to walk the streets at night," it is "criminal brutality."[20] In Detroit, the Urban League launched a community attack on crime that has attracted wide initial support among blacks and whites. One black leader spoke of the need for more policemen and sentences that "will disturb the criminal, shaking him from criminal acts."[21] In the National Opinion Research Center study of ten thousand citizens and their attitudes toward the police, black men at every income level were more likely to believe that the police were very good or pretty good at being "respectful to people like yourself" than they were to believe that the police did a very good or pretty good job at "giving protection to the people

59

in the neighborhood." In both cases, the highest-income blacks—earning over $10,000 a year—were the most critical.[22]

Contrary to what one might expect, the citizens most worried about crime are *not* those with the most favorable attitudes toward the police. In Washington, at least, blacks (and whites) with the least personal anxiety about crime had the most positive attitudes toward the police; those with the greatest anxiety had the most critical attitudes toward the police.[23]

It is hardly surprising that there should be such widespread concern among blacks over police protection. According to our best estimates, a black is almost four times as likely as a white to be the victim of a rape or a robbery and twice as likely to be the victim of an assault. (Whites, by contrast, are more likely to have things stolen from them—perhaps because they have more to be stolen.)[24]

In sum, blacks are more likely than whites to be critical of the police on grounds of both abuse and inadequate protection; while criticism of inadequate protection is voiced by close to a majority of all blacks, criticism of police abuse is expressed by a minority of perhaps a quarter to a third and experience of police abuse is confined to a very small minority; anti-police attitudes are strongest among young black males; older blacks are much less likely to report police abuses but just as likely to report inadequate protection, perhaps because an older person is less likely to come into contact with the police as a suspect but just as likely to come into contact with a criminal as his victim; and finally, there are indications of outspoken demands among older blacks for *more*, not less, police activity.

Police Views of the Citizen

The views of many police officers seem to confirm the "war" theory of police-community relations. Data gathered at least as far back as 1960 suggest that most big-city officers see the citizenry as at best uncooperative and at worst hostile. For example, a majority of Chicago police sergeants questioned in

1960 and again in 1965 felt that civilians generally did not cooperate with the police, that the department did not have the respect of most citizens, that their civilian friends would criticize the department to their faces, and that most people obey the law only from fear of being caught.[25] Recently such opinions have been expressed by leaders of various police organizations, such as the Patrolmen's Benevolent Association, and by a growing number of police chiefs.

In fact, as the previous section indicated, the majority of all citizens and the vast majority of white citizens have a generally good opinion of the police and are in favor of measures designed to help them. The apparent contradiction between actual citizen opinion and police perception of it stems, I believe, from the fact that the average patrolman in a big city is most frequently in contact, not with the "average" citizen, but with a relatively small number of persons who are heavy users of police services (willingly or unwillingly), and his view of citizen attitudes is strongly influenced by this experience. By the nature of his job, the police officer is disproportionately involved with the poor, the black, and the young—partly because young males, especially poor ones, are more likely to be involved in criminal activities and breaches of the peace and partly because even the law-abiding poor (who are, after all, the majority of the poor) must rely on the police for a variety of services that middle-class families do not require (if they do, they obtain them from non-police sources). The police, for example, are routinely expected in poor areas to deal with family quarrels; in more affluent neighborhoods, such disputes are either less threatening to the participants or are kept by them out of public view.

In a study done for the Kerner Commission, Peter H. Rossi and his colleagues at Johns Hopkins University interviewed over 400 police officers working in largely black sections of eleven major cities. When asked in general terms what they felt their major problem was, more officers mentioned a lack of public support than any other factor.[26] Fifty-four per cent were dissatisfied with the lack of respect they received from citizens; thirty per cent believed that the average citizen in these neighborhoods held them in contempt. But when the police were asked about the views of *particular groups* in the neighborhood, a different picture emerged. The vast majority (between 72 and 94 per cent) felt that older persons, storekeepers, school teachers, and whites were on their side; the police were divided as to whether most blacks saw the police as friends, as enemies, or were indifferent; a majority believed that most adolescents saw the police as enemies.[27]

Interestingly, black police officers (about a hundred were interviewed) had the same opinion as their white colleagues: to them, the chief source of hostile citizen attitudes was to be found, in increasing order of importance, among "most Negroes," "most young adults," and "most adolescents."[28] The black officers are generally more sympathetic to the problems of blacks than are white officers—they are much more likely to believe that blacks are badly treated by the city as a whole and by the police in particular—but their conception of the problems facing the police officer tends to be quite similar to that of their white colleagues.[29]

In sum, when questioned closely the community and the police tend to agree as to the source of their difficulties, though they clearly disagree over who is to blame. The chief problem is to be found in the relations between young males, especially black young males, and ghetto police officers. But if this is true, why is there not a tacit alliance between older black residents, interested in better police protection and fearful of rising rates of crime (especially juvenile crime), and police officers who are also concerned about crime and who want more cooperation in ending it? In part, there is such a convergence of views—one night spent in a ghetto police precinct will provide graphic evidence of the extent to which the older black residents, especially the women, regularly turn to the police for help. But to a considerable degree the alliance is never forged, at least not to the extent that one finds in a middle-class white suburb. The reasons are skin color and the conditions of ghetto life.

Blackness conceals, for many police officers, the important differences in social class and respectability among blacks. Because the urban lower class is today disproportionately black (just as it was once disproportionately Irish), a dark skin is to the police a statistically significant cue as to social status and thus as to potential criminality. If arrest figures are to be believed, blacks are ten times as likely to commit a murder and eight times as likely to commit an assault as whites.[30] The fact that social class and family background, not race as such, probably explain these differences in rate is less apparent than the association between skin color and crime; understandably (though often unjustly) a black skin is taken as grounds for police suspicion and therefore for questioning and frisking.

The conditions of ghetto life intensify the problem. Owing to residential segregation, blacks of many social strata, and thus of many differing degrees of law-abidingness, are forced (or seek) to live in close proximity. The territorial differentiation along lines of social class characteristic of white society is less evident among black. To the police, the heterogeneous, densely-settled ghetto makes it difficult to perceive or to act upon differences in social position. Since such a large proportion of urban blacks live in or near high-crime areas, the innocent become not only victims of crime but objects of police suspicion.

Because of skin color and residential density, blacks are more likely than whites to come into adversary contact with the police. This problem, serious in any case, becomes acute if the police feel themselves obliged to intensify their crime prevention activities. There are very few strategies by which the police can reduce crime rates—indeed, for some "private" crimes, such as murder, there is almost nothing they can do—but such strategies as they have require them to place a community under closer surveillance and thus to multiply the occasions on which citizens are likely to feel themselves unreasonably stopped, questioned, or observed. Short of assigning foot patrolmen to every street corner in order to deter crime by their mere presence, the police, facing critical manpower shortages, can only increase the rate at which they stop and question suspicious pedestrians and motorists. Inevitably, the great majority of the persons stopped will be innocent of any wrong doing and, inevitably, many of these innocent persons will believe the police are harassing them; inevitably, innocent blacks will believe that they are being harassed because of their race.

Thus, if the law-abiding majority in a black community demands more police protection, they are likely to be calling for police activity that will increase the frequency of real or perceived police abuses. If, on the other hand, they demand an end to police harassment, they are likely to be ending police practices that have some (no one knows how much) crime prevention value.

The apparent tradeoff between improved crime prevention and reduced police harassment is, of course, complicated by the quality of police behavior. Intensive, or so-called saturation, patrol may produce a minimum of incidents if each officer who stops or questions a citizen is a model of politeness, discretion, and reassurance, while even passive patrol methods may result in hostility if citizens are rudely questioned, harshly treated, or shoved, insulted, or threatened. It is important to know, therefore, how the police behave toward citizens as well as what they think of them.

To some observers, of course, it is enough to know what the police think. If the police have anti-black attitudes, they will behave in anti-black ways. Though this argument is often advanced by liberals desirous of changing the police, it is in fact nothing less than a restatement of a familiar conservative argument that "You can't legislate morality." We ought to be suspicious of such arguments wherever they are encountered for they rest on a simplistic notion of human behavior; namely, that any act is uniquely determined by the attitude of the person committing it. Such a view neglects the important ways in which society intervenes between beliefs and actions by creating a range of expectations, roles, rewards, sanctions, and constraints that powerfully influence behavior and modify the motivating power of attitudes. The proper question is, Under what circumstances will a given attitude lead to a certain behavior?

The answer to that question is all the more important given what we know of the attitudes of the police toward blacks. In a study done for the President's Commission on Law Enforcement and the Administration of Justice, observers accompanied more than 600 police officers in three cities while they went about their duties over an extended period of time. Careful records were kept of what the officers said and did. These showed that over three-fourths of the white officers working in predominantly black areas expressed "prejudiced" or "highly prejudiced" views about blacks.[31] And 28 per cent of the *black* officers assigned to these black precincts also expressed anti-black sentiments. (Interestingly, black officers assigned to racially mixed neighborhoods were *less* prejudiced against blacks.)[32] If attitudes lead directly to behavior, then the prospects for fair treatment of black citizens are bleak indeed.

But though the officers being observed in the three-city study were quite candid in expressing anti-black attitudes, there was little evidence of comparably systematic anti-black behavior. In 5,339 police-citizen encounters witnessed by commission staff members, there were only 20 where the officers used clearly excessive force, and in more than half of these cases the citizen was white.[33] As with physical force, so with verbal abuse—both were distinctive for their rarity. The police behaved in an "obviously prejudiced" way in 2 per cent of the encounters and in a somewhat prejudiced way in another 6 per cent.[34] In 11 per cent of the cases, the officer spoke in "brusque" or "hostile" manner, but even here the police did not appear to single out blacks; persons of both races were equally likely to be the objects of verbal discourtesy with the chance of such discourtesy increasing whenever the citizen was especially agitated, "disrespectful," or deviant in manner or behavior.[35]

Naturally, the presence of observers may have led many officers to alter their behavior in accordance with what was expected of them. It is impossible to measure accurately police misconduct because the measurement affects the conduct. However, three things should be borne in mind before discounting these findings altogether. First, the police clearly did not modify their *conversation* in approved directions—they spoke critically of blacks despite the presence of observers. Second, a significant number of illegal acts were committed by the police in the presence of the observers, many of them much more serious (from a legal point of view) than being harsh to blacks. And finally, even if the findings on excessive force reported to the commission are multiplied by a factor of three or four, they still account for only a very small fraction of all police-citizen contacts.

In short, there is some reason for believing that it is the *function* of the police, sometimes aggravated as much by their manner as by their use of excessive force, that creates police-community tensions. The vast majority of police-citizen contacts produce no arrests, yet the vast majority also involve police questioning of citizens. Out of over 1,800 police contacts with blacks in the three-city study, for example, the police had reason to suspect that the person they were addressing was a probable offender in about 40 per cent of the cases, yet an arrest was made in only about 10 per cent of the cases.[36] Those who were treated as suspects but who were not arrested might well feel aggrieved—that the police were "picking" on them or being "unfair"—and aggrieved because of their race. Out of 155 blacks searched by the police in the presence of observers, weapons (a gun or a knife) were found in about one-fourth of the cases.[37] To the police, such a high rate of recovery of concealed weapons amply justifies the searches; to the three-fourths who were searched though they had no weapons, the frisk might well be regarded as an insulting intrusion. If, as seems likely, certain persons—especially young males in high-crime neighborhoods—are repeatedly subject to such stops, questionings, and searches, it is easy to understand why they would develop intensely anti-police feelings.

The most dramatic allegations of systematic police attacks on blacks derive from the claim, made by a lawyer for the Black Panthers, that twenty-eight Panthers have been murdered by the police. Subsequent investigation has cast considerable doubt on this claim. The list finally produced by the lawyer contained nineteen, not twenty-eight, names. Of these, nine were not shot by the police at all—one was shot by his wife, another by a grocer whose store he was robbing, four by members of a rival black nationalist organization, and one by other Panthers; in two cases, no assailant has been identified. Of the ten shot by the police, six had first shot *at* the police and two others were involved in shootings with the police in which who fired first is in dispute. In only two cases can it be shown that law enforcement officials clearly used excessive force—the killing of Fred Hampton and Mark Clark in Chicago in December 1969—and in this case the officers were not from the Chicago police department but from the state's attorney's office.[38]

In matters of this nature, there is little likelihood that the facts will ever catch up with popular beliefs. The mass media always print but rarely investigate such charges, and, in any case, if these happen to be exaggerated or untrue, those who believe in the "genocidal" policies of the police will find other incidents or rumors to support their theories. And the police, in turn, will become increasingly convinced that their behavior will never be judged dispassionately, and therefore they might as well indulge their most cynical and intemperate sentiments. (It is worth noting that though the Chicago police department was not responsible for the raid that resulted in the deaths of Hampton and Clark, it felt compelled to engage in an investigation of the incident that a Federal grand jury publicly labelled "totally inadequate," "seriously deficient," and suggestive of "purposeful malfeasance.")[39] In no aspect of American race relations is the operation of the self-fulfilling prophecy so thoroughly and so tragically effective.

Police-Community Relations

The central finding that emerges from this review of the evidence on police-citizen contacts in ghetto situations is that the relations between police and citizens are a result of the effort of the police to attain their major objectives—crime prevention, criminal apprehension, and order maintenance. How the citizen feels about the officer results from his evaluation of the officer's performance of his principal duties under conditions such that innocence offers no protection against police intervention. In some cases, the normal friction produced by police inquiries is exacerbated by an escalation of rhetoric and threats between suspect and patrolman, each seeking to demonstrate his own self-respect and authority; in other cases tensions are heightened by the objectionable personality and manner of a particular officer. But even if *all* officers were correct in their behavior, tensions and hostile attitudes would nonetheless often result.

The chief policy implication of this argument is that police-community relations cannot be substantially improved by programs designed to deal with the citizen in settings other than encounters with patrolmen; evening meetings, discussion groups, block clubs, police-community councils, and the like will be seen by both officer and citizen as tangential to their central relationship. Nor can the behavior of patrolmen be modified other than by providing him with incentives and instructions relevant to his central task; lecturing him on good behavior, sending him to one-week human relations training institutes, or providing him with materials designed to make him think of blacks as just like everybody else will be ignored and even scorned by him.

Indeed, seeing the police-ghetto problem in the context of the central police mission and its incompatibility with the freedom of all persons to come and go as they please cannot make one optimistic about how much improvement is possible at all in police relations with blacks. So long as crime and disorder are disproportionately to be found among young lower-class males, and so long as blacks remain over-represented in (though by no means identical with) such groups, blacks—especially young ones—and the police are going to be adversaries.

Some evidence of this comes from comparative studies of the police in different cities with radically different police administrations. In one of the studies done for the President's Commission on Law Enforcement and the Administration of Justice, citizens were interviewed in two cities. One had a traditional police force with older patrolmen, a decentralized administrative structure, poor equipment and facilities, low pay, few blacks on the force, almost no community-relations program, and weak internal discipline. The other was nationally famous for its modernized, professional style; it had young patrolmen, good pay, highly centralized administration, an active internal inspection and discipline system, a large community-relations program, and a high proportion of blacks serving in the ranks. In each city, residents of a predominantly black area were interviewed. The results showed that the citizens were aware of the kind of department they had: in the city with the professionalized force, only 18 per cent thought that the police were not doing a good job, while in the city with the traditional force, 35 per cent had this view. And when storekeepers in the area were asked how fast the police would respond to a call, only 19 per cent of those in the traditional city but 40 per cent of those in the professionalized city believed the police would arrive in less than five minutes.[40]

But when asked how they evaluated the fairness, honesty, and abusiveness of the two forces, the citizens of the two communities displayed little difference in attitude. In both places, 43 per cent said that being a black makes a difference in how you are treated by the police; in both cities 10 per cent said that they had little respect for the police; in both cities, 16 per cent said they had seen the police use unnecessary force. Slightly more persons in the professionalized city (53 per cent) had "great respect" for the police than did residents of the traditional city (43 per cent), but the difference was not large.[41] The head of the professionalized department may wonder whether his efforts have been worth the candle.

The possibility of substantial improvements in police-community relations is sometimes argued by comparing, not various American cities with each other, but by contrasting American and British police forces. The London Metropolitan police constable is pictured as a man of unflappable civility, polite but firm, who carries the day by imperturbability and restraint. The difference may exist as stated, or it may have been magnified by literary exaggeration (there have been almost no studies of the "bobby".) In any case, it matters little—New York or Chicago cannot become London regardless of how large a foundation grant we obtain. The deference to authority and to such symbols of authority as the uniform and the badge that have traditionally characterized British life are not easily imported here; indeed, there is some evidence that, with the weakening of ancient distinctions of class and position and the migration into England of ethnic and racial minorities, the English are as likely to become slightly Americanized as the other way around.

The American officer's tendency to assert his *personal* authority arises from two features of American life that are beyond manipulation. First, Americans are not accustomed to playing roles that imply servility, unmanliness, or indifference to personal insults—they cannot distinguish between a challenge to the uniform and a challenge to the man wearing it. Ameri-

70

cans may be less able (in human relations terms) to be good policemen for the same reason they are less able to be good waiters. In both cases, they prefer maintaining their self-respect to keeping their self-control. Second, a British observer of the police in both countries has commented that in a culturally heterogeneous society, such as America's, "common understandings are less inclusive" and therefore the American officer "cannot rely upon the authority of his uniform" but must in addition "establish a personal authority by proving what a good guy he is, or what a dangerous one."[42] When one adds to the problem of sustaining one's authority in a divided society the ever-present fear of a violent death which confronts an American officer even in (some would say especially in) the pacification of a routine domestic quarrel, the likelihood that he will behave in a suspicious, brusque, and challenging manner is further increased.

Such gloomy views do not, of course, settle the matter. We have all had contact with police officers and most of us can recall officers who were friendly as well as a few who were rude. In the ghetto (and indeed within the police force) the identity of the few most abusive officers is widely known and they are compared unfavorably to the others who are more correct. If differences exist, why cannot they be made greater? To the extent a few "rotten apples" create tensions, then, of course, we can do something. The Law Enforcement Commission and the Kerner Commission have cited examples of officers who behaved in a hostile manner toward blacks being assigned to ghetto areas and others being left in such areas even over neighborhood complaints. Such men are known; such men can and should be reassigned.

But a further difficulty emerges. While it is possible to remove the rotten apples from sensitive areas, it is now virtually certain that the good apples will be removed, too. The ablest officers are likely to be rewarded with promotions, desirable

71

duty assignments, and better job conditions. All these steps take the best officers out of the most difficult neighborhoods and place them in quiet areas, or in headquarters, or in the detective bureau. The present reward system of the police bureaucracy tends to induce men to do those things that will get them *out* of ghetto or other difficult areas, leaving the field to the rotten apples or, at best, to the mediocre ones. A senior police officer described to me the conditions prevailing in the Watts area of Los Angeles just before the riot. Assigned to that precinct, he said, were young men on their way up, older men on their way down, and middle-aged men going nowhere. Needless to say, the men on their way up soon got up—and out.

In addition to removing the rotten apples, various measures have been proposed to improve the behavior of the majority of men who are good officers but perhaps not sufficiently diplomatic: hiring "better men," recruiting college graduates, subjecting officers to sensitivity training or other forms of intensive personality reorientations, and organizing police-community relations programs, councils, or bureaus. When so little is known about what might make a difference, all these strategies are no doubt worth trying. What needs emphasis here is that *so little is known.*

Consider measures designed to get or produce better men. The central problem is that we have not known how to define or identify a "better man" or a "good cop," and until very recently, we have not even tried to learn how.[43] In any individual case, of course, we might be able to make such a judgment but it is risky in the single instance and impossible in the mass. One pioneering study done for the Chicago police department suggests that we may be able to devise psychological tests that will predict who will make good or bad patrolmen.[44] In the study, 490 patrolmen were given four hours of tests and then had their performance evaluated by their supervisors, by the number of civilian complaints against them, and by other standards. The tests, at least when applied to black and white officers

separately, showed a significant correlation with performance.*
(Interestingly, one of the best predictors turns out to be the
family stability of the officer.) This preliminary study has yet
to be repeated in other cities and many questions still must be
answered—chiefly, the reliability of the measures of patrol performance. And even the best research into attributes can never
be wholly successful, for attributes affect behavior only in the
context of particular situations, and the interaction of attribute
and situation is exceptionally difficult to predict. Such tests
may well be useful in weeding out the poorest risks, but it is
unlikely they can guarantee the selection of officers who can
handle any situation to the satisfaction of all concerned.

In the meantime, some have argued that college-trained men
are more likely to have the desired qualities. A plausible case
can be made for this view. Even if a college teaches a man
nothing of value in police work, it has two useful side effects;
first, it selects from the general population men who have certain qualities (motivation, self-discipline, general intelligence)
that are probably quite useful in a police career and, second, it
inculcates certain characteristics (civility, urbanity, self-control)
that might be especially desired in an officer. It is a measure of
our ignorance in these matters that an equally plausible case to
the contrary can be made. Recruiting college men will no doubt
reduce substantially (at least for the time being) the chances of
adding more blacks and other minority groups to the police
forces, for they are underrepresented in college classes. Second,
college may make a man civil (though recent campus disturbances suggest its effect is not quite universal) but it also gives
him (or reenforces for him) his sense of duty. This has led some
college-trained officers to be excessively aggressive and arrest-
prone when a gentler hand might be better. Third, college men
may not be able as easily to identify with or understand prob-

*Among other things, the study found that one need not "set a thief to
catch a thief"—the best patrolmen were those with stable and cooperative
personalities, not sociopathic ones.

lems of lower- and working-class persons with whom they must deal. Finally, a police career is most unattractive for a college man—the work of a patrolman is routine, sometimes dull, frequently unpleasant, and occasionally dangerous. One study in New York City showed that patrolmen with a college education display a higher degree of cynicism and a greater sense of deprivation than those with less education.[45] In sum, the value of college training is still largely a matter of conjecture.

Better training for men on the force is always recommended. There can be little doubt that the training now received is often perfunctory, partly as a result of inadequate programs and partly as a result of the desperate need for additional men—a need that has led some departments to put rookies on the street before their academy course is completed. But even assuming lengthy preservice training, "human relations" is inevitably that part of the curriculum with the least direct effect on the policemen. The law of arrest, or first aid, or the use of weapons can be taught by lecture and demonstration, but the management of personal relations in tense situations is not so easily taught. It is the universal testimony of the officers I have interviewed that training-room discussions of minority groups and police-community relations have little impact and that such impression as they produce quickly evaporates when the officer goes on the street and first encounters hostile or suspicious behavior. The officer may remember what he is *not* supposed to do ("don't address blacks with a racially insulting name, such as 'boy' ") but he will often find other ways of asserting his personal authority short of using an obvious slur.

If conventional training methods are of little value in this area, is it possible to develop unconventional, more intensive techniques that will work a more profound change in the attitude of the officer? Some departments have experimented with sensitivity training or similar methods designed to produce a heightened self-awareness and even a significant personality change. Such methods are based on group discussions, stimulated but not directed by a training leader, in which the participants criticize one another and reexamine themselves in prolonged and often emotional sessions.[46] Sometimes only police officers participate in such sessions; in other experiments, police and blacks (or other community residents) participate together. One of the chief purposes of sensitivity training is to change the participants' attitude toward authority and its exercise so that they will engage in cooperative problem-solving, rather than struggle to win superiority or maintain personal autonomy.

Unfortunately, the effects on organizational behavior generally of such training (actually, reeducation) methods have not been carefully studied, and the effects on police organization and behavior in particular have scarcely been studied at all. Though there are many enthusiasts for these techniques, and though their enthusiasm may derive from personal experience in seeing people changed, the empirical evidence that such change can be induced in organizations as a whole on a lasting basis and without important sacrifices in other values (such as goal attainment, productivity, or equity) is at best equivocal.[47] And there are reasons to suppose that police work may be an especially refractory target for these methods. The patrolman, after all, is not regularly engaged in problem-solving with familiar colleagues in a common organization; he is engaging in enforcing the law and settling disputes among strangers, many of whom are fearful or hostile, and some of whom may be dangerous. Conflict is not a figment of either party's imagination, it is real and serious (though either party may exaggerate it and thereby unnecessarily exacerbate it). And the patrolman typically works alone, or in pairs, and not as part of supportive organizations. None of these cautionary remarks is intended to call a halt to sensitivity training, only to urge its evaluation and to prepare us for discovering that it produces at best only limited gains.

Finally, conventional police-community relations theory assigns a high priority to community organization. In many cities, the police have organized a community relations bureau with officers working either out of headquarters or precinct stations to meet with civic, minority, and neighborhood organizations and to stimulate new activities, especially those involving young people. Some departments have formed neighborhood councils or committees with which senior officers regularly meet to discuss grievances and problems. There are two quite different elements to these police-community relations strategies. One is communication—discussions, meetings, the airing of complaints, the explanation of police actions. The other is service—helping to solve community problems (even those which may not involve the police directly), remedying grievances, and handling complaints. Though each function may be performed passively and chiefly with an eye to their public relations values, when performed vigorously they lead to the development of quite different relations with the community. In the first case, the police are explaining themselves to the public, seeking to win cooperation; in the second, the police often are representing the community to (or against) the department and other city agencies. In the former instance, the police are likely to find themselves involved with middle-class (or stable working-class) families and organizations; in the second, they are likely to become involved with lower-class persons.

The communications strategy is exemplified by the activities of one large midwestern police department. A study of its district community workshops discovered that the value of such meetings depended on the character of the neighborhood. In a high-crime-rate area inhabited by both well-to-do whites living in high-rise apartments and lower-income blacks in public housing projects, a workshop meeting was well attended (about 200 people) by both whites and blacks, but all were adults—there were few young people, especially young blacks, present. There was a cooperative and constructive discussion with the police on how to solve vice and crime problems, especially those in the public housing projects. Plans were announced for assigning patrolmen to "vertical patrols" in the projects. Everyone left feeling that something useful had been accomplished.

In another neighborhood, populated by university students and poor blacks, the workshop meeting was a fiasco. The young *did* attend (about a hundred), mostly to complain about the police handling of a student anti-war demonstration. The police refused to answer questions, claiming that the matter was before the courts and thus they were enjoined from speaking about it. The blacks soon became disgusted with the haggling over the demonstration; they cared little about the war or about anti-war protest, they said, but cared greatly about the high crime rate in their neighborhood and the "disrespectful" manner of the police. The three-corner shouting match—students, police, and blacks—broke up in confusion and bitterness.

In a third district, the crime rate was low. Middle- and upper-middle-class whites and blacks lived in a peaceful community and had little interest in police issues. Only thirty persons appeared for the workshop meeting and few raised any crime or police issues. There were complaints, but not ones the police could respond to—garbage collection, parking regulations, dogs running loose. Few community leaders were in attendance; most of the audience was composed of chronic complainers, each of whom was irritated by the need to sit through everybody else's account of *his* problem. The meeting ended with little sense of accomplishment.[48]

That the workshop strategy worked well in one district suggests that it is worth doing; that it did not work well in two others indicates that its limits should be clearly recognized. (Some persons, of course, will argue that it is of no value at all if it only reaches middle-class persons, especially adults, but it is hard to understand why the concern of adults for more police protection is any less worthy of being served than the concern of young people for less police abuse.) Efforts to reach the young and the lower-income groups, at least by the communications approach, are exceptionally difficult and perhaps impossible. One first-hand account of such an effort is typical of many. A group of young black "street corner" males was enrolled in a job-preparation program in a West Coast city. As the author

77

describes it, the men were cool—they spoke in the hip vernacular, wore sun glasses indoors, and were dressed in loud (but inexpensive) clothes. Most were school dropouts. Many had police records. They were paid five dollars a day to be in the training program.

Almost daily the men spoke of police brutality. All wanted to meet a representative of the police. One finally came, a sergeant from the community relations bureau. He was almost immediately put down, with angry questions about "why you cats always kicking cats' asses" and detailed personal horror stories of experiences with the police that each had had. The sergeant could not get in a word. The next day, a deputy chief appeared to try his hand at improving "communications." He, too, was besieged with stories of alleged brutality. He asked the men if they had filed complaints; none had. The chief asked why not. The men responded that if they did, "we would just get our asses kicked harder by the cop next time." The chief insisted that complaints would be fairly investigated. The men were not satisfied. One asked,

"Okay man, you pretty smart. If I smack my buddy here upside the head and he files a complaint, what you gonna do?"

"Arrest you," the chief replied.

"Cool. Now let's say one of your ugly cops smacks *me* upside the head and I file a complaint—what you gonna do?"

"Investigate the complaint," the chief said. If it were true, the police would take action and probably suspend the officer.

"Well," the black rejoined, "how come *we* get arrested and *you* only get investigated?"

Efforts to distinguish between the private resort to violence, for which there is no justification, and official use of violence, for which there may be, were to no avail. The chief was shouted down and finally left in disgust.[49]

Better designed or more protracted efforts might in fact produce more constructive communication between hip young black males and the police, but the gains, however worthwhile, are likely to be slight, for the problem is not fundamentally one of communication. There is genuine conflict between the youths, who want to be left alone, and the police, who regard their antagonists (rightly) as the chief source of crime and disorder and who seek by various means, some proper and some improper, to control them—often on behalf of older blacks who want better police protection.

But communication is not the only strategy the police might follow. On occasion—San Francisco is a leading example—they have developed instead a service approach with young black males as the clients. Begun in 1959, the Police Community Relations Unit was seen by its first commander, Dante Andreotti, as a means of getting some officers to identify with and act on behalf of inner-city residents.[50] Thirteen men work in the unit; five are assigned to the neighborhood headquarters of anti-poverty agencies, and the rest work with youth gangs, the high schools, hippies, and other problem populations. Most of their time is spent with teenagers and young adults providing a range of services, such as opening up recreation opportunities to gangs and helping find jobs. But increasingly, the PCR efforts involved the unit in helping blacks and others deal with the police. The unit has sought to help young men overcome the disabilities of an arrest record and has advised them how to bring complaints against police officers for misconduct.

This service strategy has meant that a new kind of communications problem now exists, arising out of the hostility between the PCR and other parts of the San Francisco police department. By urging young men and their prospective employers not to take too seriously arrest records, the PCR was, in the eyes of other officers, "belittling the significance of arrests" in a way that seemed to amount to a "nullification of police efforts."[51] Aiding citizens in filing complaints against the police appeared to be a direct challenge to the force and as a result, PCR officers are not even on speaking terms with some of their nominal colleagues in other parts of the force.

Owing to this conflict, the PCR has had a checkered history depending, it would seem, on the vigor of the officer leading it and the support it received from the chief and the mayor. Assessing its effectiveness in the community is hazardous—its partisans strongly support it, its members are typically loyal and enthusiastic, and some observers credit it with having eased tensions and improved community relations. On the other hand, there has been a major riot in San Francisco, the Black Panthers are active, and San Francisco State College is hardly tranquil. What is clear is that the service strategy has brought at least some police officers into closer contact with the young blacks than has any discussion-oriented communications strategy. And the fact that the PCR has produced conflict within the force is not in itself sufficient reason for discrediting it—many large organizations must learn to live with intra-bureau tensions and some may profit from the improved flow of information and the creation of policy options that results.

Better Management of the Patrol Function
Though some or all of the methods described above for improving police-community relations may be useful and a few may be essential, the major problem facing a city wishing to make progress in this area is to devise ways of improving the way in which the police perform their central function—patrolling to prevent crime, preserve order, and enforce laws. There are, however, important limits to the improvements that can be made because the nature of the patrol function is such as to deny to the police administrator (and perforce to the community) the opportunity to exercise close and meaningful control over the behavior of patrolmen who work alone or in pairs, out of sight of their superiors, and in an environment that requires them to enter into social conflicts among persons who do not always concede the legitimacy of police authority. This is especially true when the police-citizen contact is initiated by the officer,

80

as when he stops a vehicle for speeding or because its occupants appear suspicious, when he questions a person on the street, or when he tells a group of young men hanging around a street corner to move on.[52]

Though it is hard to control the officer's conduct when the discretion he has in deciding whether and how to intervene is necessarily great, some gain can be had by recognizing that the crime-prevention and order-maintenance functions of the patrolman are the essence of his task. Community tensions are less likely to be aggravated by the arrest of a known felon or the interdiction of a serious crime in progress than they are by the management of seemingly minor incidents—a traffic stop, a street questioning, or a tavern brawl. This implies that judging patrolmen by their arrest records (or by the number of traffic citations issued) is not the appropriate grounds for rewarding (and thus influencing) police behavior. Furthermore, the officers best able to manage their beat in order to prevent crime and keep order should not be rewarded in ways that take these officers out of difficult districts (or out of patrol work altogether). The police will be able to perform their major task better if they have reliable and detailed information about the character and habits of the persons whose public conduct they are supervising. Finally, it seems clear that the proper performance of the patrol functions is time consuming and therefore costly in terms of manpower. To learn enough about a neighborhood to patrol it intelligently, to spend enough time with street-corner youths to keep their conduct within acceptable limits without relying on gruff orders to disperse, to display a police presence on the streets with sufficient frequency and persistence to deter the commission of street crimes—all of these tasks require the deployment of large numbers of officers in close contact with residents and store owners. Good patrol work, good police protection, and better police-community relations are not inexpensive or amenable to new technologies.

If this perspective is correct, then a number of specific policy proposals come to mind. First, big-city police departments with serious crime and community-relations problems require substantial increases in patrol manpower. There is some evidence that saturation foot patrol will reduce the rate of street crime and increase the probability of arresting those who commit street crimes that go undeterred.[53] There is also evidence that attempting to handle street crime with insufficient manpower unfortunately means putting officers in patrol cars and directing them either to respond only to radio dispatches (i.e., wait until a crime has occurred) or to stop suspicious strangers in hopes of preventing crimes. But this tactic, while understandable given the manpower and money shortages of many departments, is regrettable both in terms of crime prevention and community relations. Unable to prevent crimes by their presence, the police seek to prevent them by aggressive investigation; unable to learn enough about a community to manage it informally, the police are required to rely on radio dispatches and to manage it formally, by arrests.

But to ask for more manpower is one thing; to find it is something else. Departments are now undermanned and often forced to accept applicants with only minimal qualifications; recruiting among certain groups (e.g., blacks, college graduates, persons with useful technical specialties) is especially difficult. Salary increases—at least of the magnitude most cities can afford—have not produced a flood of new recruits. If the number and quality of police personnel are crucial to any major improvement in police work, more drastic steps than any now taken must be contemplated. There are two alternatives. One would be to raise police salaries, especially for patrolmen, by such a large amount (up to $15,000 a year) that police work would be attractive despite its obvious burdens. Increases of this magnitude would require state and federal aid to the cities in amounts far beyond that now authorized and would in addition require the ending of statutory restrictions on the amount of federal aid that can be used to pay police salaries.*

The second possibility is to make police service an alternative to (or a part of) military service. Making police service an alternative to military service for those who are drafted would not only bring in large numbers of additional men (perhaps for three-year tours of duty), but it would also rotate through police departments men who ordinarily have no contact with and perhaps little respect for the police, such as blacks, college men, and the like. Obviously, such a proposal would require major changes in the way the police are now administered. Men opting for police service would have to be carefully screened for competence (somehow defined) and assigned to the states or localities on a quota system; departments eligible to receive drafted recruits would have to meet minimum standards for training, manpower administration, and pay and benefits; draftees would have to be given, at the end of their required tour of duty, an option to reenlist and thus continue to serve in the police (voluntarily) on a par with other professional officers. These changes may be more than can be accomplished in our decentralized police system. The advantages of selective service recruitment is not only that it would provide more manpower than we are able to hire, but also that the increases would be temporary—we could cut back when crime and community relations problems have eased. And short-term civilian members would help create a civilian perspective in the police as well as giving it a cross section of skills and backgrounds that can be utilized.

Whatever method is selected for augmenting the size of the force, equal attention must be paid to its deployment. Centrally

*According to the *Omnibus Crime Control and Safe Streets Act of 1968* (Public Law 351, 90th Congress), not more than one-third of any grant for law enforcement may be used for the compensation of personnel (section 301[d]).

dispatched patrol cars answering calls throughout a city or borough is an economical form of deployment, but it may not be efficient in terms of either crime prevention or community relations. Saturation foot patrol is extremely costly, but seems to have deterrent value as well as the value of familiarizing the officer with a neighborhood on a non-adversary basis. Opening a large number of store-front police service offices would give more citizens access to police attention without building expensive precinct houses complete with jails, squad rooms, and communications facilities. Even better (but probably much harder to achieve) would be inducing some patrolmen to live in the neighborhoods they police. Money or other incentives would have to be provided to compensate them for the costs of such residence, including the greater risk of becoming a victim of a crime, and given the attitudes that exist now the incentive might probably have to be a large one.

Instituting a service-oriented community relations unit may be desirable even if it generates intradepartmental tensions. It would be important, however, not to isolate it from the rest of the force or staff it wholly with officers who make it a career and thus enter into permanent hostility with other patrolmen. Officers should be rotated through it, after suitable training, on perhaps three or four years tours of duty.

Perhaps of greater importance than what service the police offer to the community is what attitude the community has toward the police. Invariably in discussions of police-community relations, spokesmen critical of police behavior insist that it is up to the police to change and that, if they do change, things will be better; spokesmen for the police, on the other hand, say that little will improve unless the citizens show more respect for law enforcement. Rarely does either side, and especially the latter, offer any concrete proposals for producing these changes. In fact, the police acting alone, whatever changes they make, cannot show much progress in community relations.

Whatever their numbers, whatever their deployment, whatever their services, to the extent they encounter a hostile or indifferent citizenry, they will be inclined to respond in kind. The mobilization of an active partnership between citizens and the police, especially in ghetto areas, is central to any substantial progress in easing tensions.

A number of proposals have been made, and a few have been tried, for so-called citizen security patrols as adjuncts to the police in high-crime areas. It is too early to tell precisely what organizational arrangements or duty assignments are optimal for such an enterprise, but it is already clear that two extreme cases can and should be avoided. One is vigilantism—volunteers exercising full police powers with no police disciplines and few legal constraints. The other is the anti-police patrol—a community organization created independently of and in opposition to the police and serving as a roving check on its behavior. The former pattern may produce oppressive and unfair practices, the latter will probably worsen police-citizen relations by bringing the two groups into organized, rather than unorganized, opposition.

It should be possible to design a collaborative venture between a volunteer citizens' group and the regular force such that the citizens work with the police, equipping them with more eyes and ears and providing whatever additional deterrent power is created by having men in appropriate helmets and insignia walking the streets or riding in cars. We do not know how many street crimes can be prevented by displaying a greater police presence on the streets, especially if the "police" are in fact local residents doing volunteer work; answering that question ought to be one of the first objects of an experimental project. But even if there are few gains in crime prevention, citizen involvement may nonetheless be useful. The police will have some tangible sign of citizen support (more tangible and certainly more useful than bumper stickers); the citizens will have a chance to help the police distinguish between (outwardly similar) troublemakers and peaceful adolescents and deal with potentially disorderly situations in ways that do not lead to curt and summary instructions to "get moving."

One experiment with a community patrol corps in Harlem occurred in 1968 and was evaluated by the Bureau of Applied Social Research at Columbia University. The results were tentative but encouraging. Though the experiment was too short (one week) and too small (thirty-eight young men, mostly black) to have any visible effect on the crime rate, the corps was successful in peacefully breaking up fights and quarrels on the street, assisting drunks, discovering and reporting hazardous building and sanitary conditions, and providing escort services to women fearful of walking home at night. The corps members, as well as a random sample of Harlem residents who were interviewed, expressed enthusiasm for the program and wished that it could continue. Though some police officers were skeptical or critical of the corps, the senior officers in charge of the experiment were on the whole pleased with the results and the potential. Problems of breaches of discipline and insufficient training arose but appeared to be amenable to correction in any long-term effort.[54] In sum, this experiment, initiated by the Vera Institute of Justice, ought to be tried on a larger scale, for a longer period, and in a number of cities.

Neighborhood involvement in law enforcement need not be limited to security patrols. Community groups can play important roles in helping take responsibility for persons awaiting trial (guaranteeing their appearance without having to make bail, finding jobs for those able to work but out of work at the time of their arrest) and in re-integrating into the community persons released from correctional institutions (by organizing, for example, halfway houses). Indeed, since the conditions of public order and the maintenance of good relations with the police are one of the chief concerns of central-city neighborhoods, it is somewhat surprising that those neighborhood organizations that arise so rarely devote themselves to action in this area (or when they do deal with law enforcement matters, it is only by making demands on the police). The problems in police-community relations will be lessened neither by making demands nor by holding discussions; they will only be meliorated (in principle, they cannot be solved) when citizen organizations and the police engage in collaborative action efforts.

Unfortunately, the obstacles to such collaboration are not solely to be found among the citizens. Increasingly, some police spokesmen have opposed citizen involvement in law enforcement, especially citizen security patrols. (These are usually the same officers that most vehemently denounce the lack of citizen cooperation and respect.) It is easy to understand why some officers should be fearful of innovations of this sort—they sometimes appear to be efforts at neighborhood control of or spying on the police. Yet that need not be the case, though it is clear that a good deal of trial and error will be necessary before anyone can say confidently what *will* be the case.

The issue of community control of the police has of late come to dominate any discussion of police-community relations, just as a few years ago such a discussion focused largely on civilian review boards. The argument increasingly heard in black areas is that both better police protection and better police conduct can only be insured by giving neighborhoods control over their own police. In this way, the police will be responsive to the needs of the local citizens; the community will develop both policies for the exercise of police discretion and methods for the restraint or correction of police misconduct.

It is difficult to evaluate this policy since, to a great extent, it is a slogan rather than a proposal, an ideology rather than a program. Its adherents believe fervently in it without being able to offer a very clear understanding of what might be involved. And since shifting authority over the police from city hall to the neighborhoods is perhaps the most far-reaching change that could be made in police practice, it is especially important that one examine it closely. Community control could vary from having neighborhood groups choose, or consent to the choice of, the police captain assigned to their precincts; to the creation of neighborhood police policy boards that would exercise day-to-day supervision over the policies and actions of officers assigned to a particular locale; and beyond to organizing the neighborhood so that it could hire, train, and deploy its own independent police force. And the range of control could vary from control over local beat patrolmen (leaving specialized units, such as traffic or even the detectives, centrally managed) to control overall aspects of police work in the area.

Whatever the form of the community-control proposals, however, certain questions can be asked that are generally applicable.[55] The first, and perhaps the most important, is whether in a period of exceptional tension between whites and blacks living in central cities, the various neighborhoods making up those cities should be given control over their own police forces. If any one neighborhood obtains control over its police, all other neighborhoods will be able to make similar demands. In a period of civil disorder, the prospects for peace are not likely to be enhanced by balkanizing the city, equipping each area with its own police force, and letting the disputants, thus armed, settle their differences as best they can.

Second, the question of community control assumes that the "community" exists and its will can be made effective in police matters. But "the community" is an abstraction; communities do not govern; particular men and factions govern. It is evident that in many central-city neighborhoods, the most active and influential factions are those most inclined to exacerbate and exploit interracial tensions, assert the most extravagant claims, and harass in the rawest manner the employees of whatever government agency operates in that area. Such factions are by no means representative of community opinion and yet so far they tend to dominate discussions and preempt the leading positions. Rank-and-file citizens with more sober and genuine concerns over crime and police behavior may not be brought to power by community control; quite the contrary, their voices may be the ones to be silenced rather than amplified.

Finally, plunging the police into a political arena in which the most emotional and provincial concerns set the tone for decision making is not likely to ease the problem of recruiting and holding able men for the force. A major concern of the patrolman arises from the inconsistent expectations and contrary authorities that now define his task; his superiors, "politicians," the public all provide him with various and conflicting definitions of his function, usually (it seems to him) by criticism after the fact. Subordinating him to community councils that regularly and variously debate his role is not likely to increase his sense of confidence or the attractiveness of a police career.

But improvements in police-community relations do not require us to choose between defending the present structure or abandoning it in favor of untested proposals for community control. The middle ground, and the one urged in this paper, is to devise strategies whereby the self-interest of both the police and the community can be enlisted in efforts to deal simultaneously and jointly with the problem of crime and community relations. The patrolman wants support, cooperation, and information; the community (or most of the community, wants greater safety, quicker, and fairer police responses, and less harshness in tone and manner. Increasing substantially the number of foot patrolmen, and doing so by using both short-term recruits and civilian auxiliaries, may well reduce street crime and draw closer together the police and the community. The community's contribution to police policy making will grow out of a collaborative relationship established to attain common goals.

Even under the best of circumstances, however, there are limits to how much can be done. There is a fundamental, and to a degree inescapable, conflict between strategies designed to cut street crime (saturation patrols, close surveillance) and those designed to minimize tensions (avoid "street shops," reduce surveillance, ignore youth groups). Ultimately the best way to minimize tensions is to find non-police methods for reducing street crime. To the extent that speedier court dispositions, more effective sentencing decisions, and improved correctional methods can reduce street crime by removing or rehabilitating repeat offenders, the burdens on the police and the tensions between police and citizen can be greatly reduced. There is some evidence that important progress can be made in these areas.[56] Though it must be said that society thus far has been most reluctant to provide support for such efforts, preferring to think of the "crime problem" as chiefly a "police problem". In the long run, general social progress, especially the reduction of poverty and unemployment, may both reduce crime rates and ease tensions between the police and those persons who, because of their class position, are the natural objects of police suspicion. In the short run, however, progress may well produce even higher crime rates (social change, by altering expectations and weakening traditional controls, always seems to have an unstabilizing effect, at least initially) and even greater mutual resentment between young men and patrolmen.

notes

Chapter 1. The Police Role in an Urban Society (pages 1-11)

1. William A. Westley, "Learning to Love the Police," *The New York Times* (November 15, 1971), p. 41. © 1971 by The New York Times Company. Reprinted by permission. Westley is director of the Industrial Relations Center, McGill University, Quebec, Canada, and author of *Violence and the Police: A Sociological Study of Law, Custom, and Morality* (Cambridge, Mass., MIT Press, 1970).

Chapter 2. Police Identity and the Police Role (pages 12-50)

1. Jesse Rubin and Daniel Cruse, "The Influence of Fatigue, Stress, and Personality on Police Operations" (report in preparation). This work was supported by the Law Enforcement Assistance Administration, U.S. Department of Justice.
2. Ellen Ferris, "The Miami Police-Community Interaction Program: An Evaluation" (report in preparation). This work was supported by the Miami Model Cities Program.
3. Erik H. Erikson, *Childhood and Society*, 2nd ed. (New York: Norton, 1963).
4. *Ibid.*, pp. 261-262.

91

5. Arthur Niederhoffer, *Behind the Shield* (Garden City, N.Y.: Double-day, 1967), p. 103. Chief William Parker, of the Los Angeles Police Department, is quoted in an interview with Donald McNamara.
6. *Ibid.*, pp. 103–151.
7. Joseph Matarazzo and others, "Characteristics of Successful Police-man and Fireman Applicants," *Journal of Applied Psychology*, Vol. 48, No. 2 (1964), pp. 123–133.
8. Robert Mills, "Use of Diagnostic Small Groups in Police Recruitment, Selection, and Training," *Journal of Criminal Law, Criminology, and Police Science*, Vol. 60, No. 2 (1969), p. 240.
9. Nelson A. Watson and James W. Sterling, *Police and Their Opinions* (Washington, D.C.: International Association of Chiefs of Police, 1969), p. 9.
10. Clifton Rhead and others, "The Psychological Assessment of Police Candidates," *American Journal of Psychiatry*, Vol. 124 (1968), pp. 1575–1580. Copyright © 1968 by the American Psychiatric Association.
11. Nelson A. Watson and James W. Sterling, *op. cit.*, p. 63.
12. James Q. Wilson, *Varieties of Police Behavior* (Cambridge, Mass,: Harvard University Press, 1968), pp. 24, 29.
13. *Ibid.*, pp. 29–30.
14. Arthur Niederhoffer, *op. cit.*, pp. 18–19.
15. Charles B. Saunders, *Upgrading the American Police* (Washington, D.C.: Brookings Institution, 1970), p. 122.
16. U.S. President's Commission on Law Enforcement and the Adminis-tration of Justice, *Task Force Report: The Police* (Washington, D.C.: U.S. Government Printing Office) 1967, p. 138.
17. Charles B. Saunders, *op. cit.*, pp. 47–48.
18. Arthur Niederhoffer, *op. cit.*, pp. 52–53. Copyright © 1967 by Arthur Niederhoffer. Reprinted by permission of Doubleday & Com-pany, Inc.
19. For a brief and informative history of policing and the police role, see U.S. President's Commission on Law Enforcement and the Adminis-tration of Justice, *op. cit.*, pp. 3–7.
20. James S. Campbell and others, *Law and Order Reconsidered: Report of the Task Force on Law and Law Enforcement to the National Commission on the Causes and Prevention of Violence* (New York: Bantam Books, 1970), p. 286.
21. James Q. Wilson, *op. cit.*, pp. 142–143.
22. James S. Campbell and others, *op. cit.*, p. 286.
23. James Q. Wilson, *op. cit.*, p. 4.

24. James S. Campbell and others, *op. cit.*, p. 291.
25. James Q. Wilson, *op. cit.*, p. 18.
26. Irving A. Wallach, *Police Function in a Negro Community* (McLean, Va.: Research Analysis Corporation, 1970), Vol. 1, p. 6.
27. Bernard L. Garmire, "Operation Impact, A Report Delivered Before the Commission of the City of Miami" (July 22, 1971).
28. Philip Solomon and Susan T. Kleeman, "Sensory Deprivation," *American Journal of Psychiatry*, Vol. 127 (1971), pp. 122–123.
29. Woodburn Heron, "The Pathology of Boredom," *Scientific American*, Vol. 196 (1957), p. 52.
30. John Zubek and others, "Perceptual Changes After Prolonged Sensory Isolation," *Canadian Journal of Psychiatry*, Vol. 15 (1961), p. 83.
31. William A. Westley, "Violence and the Police," *American Journal of Sociology*, Vol. 59 (1953). Reprinted by permission of the University of Chicago Press.
32. Nelson A. Watson and James W. Sterling, *op. cit.*, p. 100.
33. Keith Bergstrom, personal communication.
34. Nelson A. Watson and James W. Sterling, *op. cit.*, p. 73.
35. James Q. Wilson, *op. cit.*, pp. 281–282.
36. Arthur Niederhoffer, *op. cit.*, p. 12
37. Frank C. Hughes, "A Policeman Comments," *The New York Times Magazine* (July 11, 1971), p. 2. © 1971 by The New York Times Company. Reprinted by permission.
38. "The Black Cop: A Man Caught in the Middle," *Newsweek* (August 16, 1971), p. 19.
39. Bernard L. Garmire, personal communication.
40. Irving A. Wallach, *op. cit.*, p. 9.
41. Joseph Edwards, personal communication. Edwards is director of the Miami Police-Community Interaction Program.
42. Sidney Epstein, "Applied Behavioral Research in Police Personnel Problems," speech at Midwestern Psychological Association (May 5, 1971).
43. Morton Bard, "The Role of Law Enforcement in the Helping System," *Community Mental Health Journal*, Vol. 7, No. 2 (June 1971), pp. 151–159.
44. *Ibid.*
45. Bernard L. Garmire, "Police Strategies for the Twentieth Century, A Report to the Miami City Commission" (March 25, 1971).
46. Robert Knight, personal communication.
47. William H. Thweatt, "A Vocational Counseling Approach to Police Selection" (University of Arizona).

48. Melany E. Baehr and others, *Psychological Assessment of Patrolmen Qualifications in Relation to Field Performance* (Washington, D.C.: U.S. Government Printing Office, 1968), pp. 230–231. This was a project of the Law Enforcement Assistance Administration, U.S. Department of Justice.
49. *Ibid.*
50. Sidney Epstein, *op. cit.*

Chapter 3. The Police in the Ghetto (pages 51–90)

1. *New York Times* (August 27, 1970), p. 1.
2. Gary T. Marx, *Protest and Prejudice* (New York: Harper & Row, 1967), p. 36.
3. Philip H. Ennis, *Criminal Victimization in the United States* (Washington, D.C.: U.S. Government Printing Office, 1967), p. 56. This research study was prepared under a grant to the National Opinion Research Center, University of Chicago, and submitted to the President's Commission on Law Enforcement and the Administration of Justice.
4. U.S. President's Commission on Law Enforcement and the Administration of Justice, *Task Force Report: The Police*, p. 146.
5. Albert D. Biderman and others, *Report on a Pilot Study in the District of Columbia on Victimization and Attitudes Toward Law Enforcement* (Washington, D.C.: U.S. Government Printing Office, 1967), p. 145. This research study was conducted under a contract to the Bureau of Social Science Research and submitted to the President's Commission on Law Enforcement and the Administration of Justice.
6. Charles H. McCaghy and others, "Public Attitudes Toward City Police in a Middle-Sized Northern City," *Criminologica*, Vol. 6 (May 1968).
7. Albert J. Reiss, Jr., "Public Perceptions and Recollections About Crime, Law Enforcement, and Criminal Justice," in *Studies in Crime and Law Enforcement in Major Metropolitan Areas* (Washington, D.C.: U.S. Government Printing Office, 1967), Vol. 1, Sec. 2, p. 55. This research study was prepared under a grant to the University of Michigan and submitted to the President's Commission on Law Enforcement and the Administration of Justice.
8. Angus Campbell and Howard Schuman, "Racial Attitudes in Fifteen American Cities," in *Supplemental Studies for the National Advisory Commission on Civil Disorders* (Washington, D.C.: U.S. Government Printing Office, 1968), pp. 41–45.

9. Albert J. Reiss, Jr., *op. cit.*, p. 52.
10. Albert D. Biderman and others, *op. cit.*, p. 138.
11. Philip H. Ennis, *op. cit.*, p. 58.
12. *Ibid.*, pp. 56, 58.
13. Albert D. Biderman and others, *op. cit.*, p. 139.
14. Albert J. Reiss, Jr., *op. cit.*, p. 52. See also Albert D. Biderman and others, *op. cit.*, p. 138.
15. U.S. President's Commission on Law Enforcement and the Administration of Justice, *op. cit.*, p. 147.
16. Angus Campbell and Howard Schuman, *op. cit.*, p. 44.
17. *Ibid.*
18. U.S. President's Commission on Law Enforcement and the Administration of Justice, *op. cit.*, p. 148.
19. Roger Beardwood, "The New Negro Mood," *Fortune*, Vol. 77, No. 1 (January 1968), p. 148.
20. Maurice Carroll, "N.A.A.C.P. Deplores Harlem 'Terror,' " *The New York Times* (December 13, 1968), pp. 1, 39.
21. Berl Falbaum, "Hundreds Join War on Crime," *The Detroit News* (February 25, 1969), p. 3-A.
22. Philip H. Ennis, *op. cit.*, pp. 55-56.
23. Albert D. Biderman and others, *op. cit.*, p. 140.
24. U.S. President's Commission on Law Enforcement and the Administration of Justice, *Task Force Report: Crime and Its Impact—An Assessment*, p. 80.
25. James Q. Wilson, "Police Morale, Reform, and Citizen Respect: The Chicago Case," in David J. Bordua, ed., *The Police* (New York: Wiley, 1967), p. 17. See also Jerome H. Skolnick, *Justice Without Trial* (New York: Wiley, 1966), pp. 9-65.
26. Peter H. Rossi and others, "Between White and Black: The Faces of American Institutions in the Ghetto," in *Supplemental Studies for the National Advisory Commission on Civil Disorders*, p. 104.
27. *Ibid.*, p. 106. See also David H. Bayley and Harold Mendelsohn, *Minorities and the Police* (New York: Free Press, 1969), pp. 45-46.
28. Peter H. Rossi and others, *op. cit.*, p. 106.
29. *Ibid.*, pp. 109, 111.
30. This was calculated from Table 31 in U.S. Federal Bureau of Investigation, *Uniform Crime Reports—1967* (Washington, D.C.: U.S. Government Printing Office, 1968), p. 126.
31. Donald J. Black and Albert J. Reiss, Jr., "Patterns of Behavior in Police and Citizen Transactions," in *Studies in Crime and Law Enforcement in Major Metropolitan Areas*, Vol. 2, Sec. 1, p. 136.
32. *Ibid.*, p. 135.

33. U.S. President's Commission on Law Enforcement and the Administration of Justice, *Task Force Report: The Police*, p. 182.
34. Donald J. Black and Albert J. Reiss, Jr., *op. cit.*, p. 42.
35. *Ibid.*, pp. 32–36.
36. *Ibid.*, p. 76.
37. *Ibid.*, p. 87.
38. This analysis of the "Panther murders" was made available from an unpublished study by Edward J. Epstein, Department of Political Science, Massachusetts Institute of Technology.
39. *Report of the January 1970 Grand Jury* (U.S. District Court, Northern District of Illinois, Eastern Division), pp. 121–123.
40. Albert J. Reiss, Jr., *op. cit.*, pp. 20, 39.
41. *Ibid.*, pp. 39, 47, 55, 75. For a more extensive and sophisticated analysis of intercity differences in public attitudes toward the police (with conclusions that suggest such differences may be significant), see Howard Schuman and Barry Gruenberg, "City as an Explanatory Variable in the Study of Racial Attitudes," (Ann Arbor: University of Michigan, Survey Research Center, 1969).
42. Michael Banton, *The Policeman and the Community* (London: Tavistock, 1964), p. 168.
43. Richard H. Blum, ed., *Police Selection* (Springfield, Ill.: Thomas, 1964), pp. 101–102.
44. Melany E. Baehr and others, *op. cit.*
45. Arthur Niederhoffer, *op. cit.*, p. 235.
46. Herbert A. Shepard, "Changing Interpersonal and Intergroup Relations in Organization," in James G. March, ed. *Handbook of Organizations* (Chicago: Rand McNally, 1965), pp. 1132–1141.
47. Harold J. Leavitt, "Applied Organizational Change in Industry," in James G. March, ed., *op. cit.*, p. 1167.
48. Charles Sklarsky, "The Police-Community Relations Program" (Cambridge, Mass.: Harvard University, Department of Government, 1968).
49. David Wellman, "Putting on the Poverty Program" (Ann Arbor: Radical Education Project, no date).
50. Mary Ellen Leary, "The Trouble with Troubleshooting," *The Atlantic* (March 1969), pp. 94–99.
51. *Ibid.*, p. 97.
52. James Q. Wilson, *Varieties of Police Behavior*, chapters 2–3.
53. James Q. Wilson, "Crime and Law Enforcement," in Kermit Gordon, ed., *Agenda for the Nation* (Washington, D.C.: Brookings Institution, 1968), pp. 179–206. See especially the account of "Operation 25" of the New York City Police Department, p. 187.

54. George Nash and others, "The Community Patrol Corps: A Descriptive Evaluation of the One-Week Experiment" (New York: Columbia University, Bureau of Applied Social Research, 1968). This report was prepared for the New York City Mayor's Criminal Justice Coordinating Council. See also Terry Ann Knopf, *Youth Patrols: An Experiment in Community Participation* (Waltham, Mass.: Brandeis University, Lemberg Center for the Study of Violence, 1969).
55. James Q. Wilson, *Varieties of Police Behavior*, pp. 288–290.
56. James Q. Wilson, "Crime and Law Enforcement," pp. 190–196. See also U.S. President's Commission on Law Enforcement and the Administration of Justice, *Task Force Report: Corrections.*

notes on contributors

BERNARD L. GARMIRE started his police career as an Indiana State Police trooper in 1937 and was chief of police in Eau Claire (Wisconsin) and Tucson before taking command of the Miami police in 1969. He has served on the faculty of the University of Arizona and has also lectured on police administration at the Federal Bureau of Investigation National Academy and at various universities and police institutes. Chief Garmire was treasurer of the International Association of Chiefs of Police and has been a consultant to the President's Commission on Campus Unrest (Scranton Commission) and to Attorneys General Ramsey Clark and John N. Mitchell. He is the author of numerous articles in professional journals on police science and administration.

JESSE G. RUBIN, M.D., is president and member of the board of the Psychiatric Institute Foundation in Washington (D.C.). He received his medical degree at the Yale University School of Medicine in 1957, served on the staff of the Baltimore City Hospitals, and then returned to Yale to study psychiatry, becoming chief resident at the Yale Psychiatric Institute in 1961. Dr. Rubin also served as staff psychiatrist in the U.S. Air Force with the rank of captain. He is associate clinical professor on the faculty of George Washington University and consultant to the department of psychology at American University. He has contributed clinical studies in psychosomatic medicine to medical journals, is editor (with Richard C. Allen and Elyce Z. Ferster) of *Readings in Law and Psychiatry*, and is preparing a textbook on group therapy.

ROBERT F. STEADMAN received his doctorate in political science at the University of Chicago in 1928 and served for seventeen years on the faculty of the Maxwell Graduate School of Citizenship and Public Affairs at Syracuse University. While on the faculty of Wayne State University from 1947 to 1956, he served as controller and head of the department of administration of the Michigan state government. Prof. Steadman was also a vice-president of the American Management Association and economic adjustment adviser in the Department of Defense. He joined CED as staff director for Improvement of Management in Government in 1963. His writings include *Public Health Organization in the Region of Chicago* and *Administration for Research*, Volume 3 of the Report of the President's Scientific Research Board.

JAMES Q. WILSON is professor of government on the faculty of arts and sciences at Harvard University and also teaches at the John F. Kennedy School of Government. He completed his graduate work at the University of Chicago in 1959 and was director of the Joint Center for Urban Studies of Harvard and the Massachusetts Institute of Technology from 1963 to 1966. Prof. Wilson served on the Sloan Commission on Cable Communications and is on the board of directors of the Police Foundation. He is a fellow of the American Academy of Arts and Sciences and a member of the National Research Council, and was awarded a Guggenheim fellowship in 1970 for a study of the nature and behavior of political organizations. Among his most recent books are *Urban Renewal: The Record and the Controversy, Varieties of Police Behavior,* and *City Politics and Public Policy.*

index

101

index

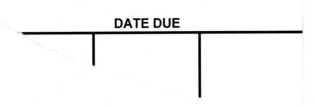

DATE DUE

THE JOHNS HOPKINS UNIVERSITY PRESS

This book was composed in Press Roman text with Helvetica display
by Jones Composition Company from a design by Laurie Jewell.
It was printed on 55-lb. Sebago Antique by Universal Lithographers, Inc.
and bound in Interlaken Matte cloth by L. H. Jenkins.